WHAT'S COOKING
Indian

Shehzad Husain

THUNDER BAY
P·R·E·S·S

Published by
Thunder Bay Press
5880 Oberlin Drive, Suite 400
San Diego, California 92121
1–800–284–3580

http://www.advmkt.com

Husain, Shehzad.
    What's Cooking Indian / Shehzad Husain.
       p. cm.
    Includes index.
    ISBN 1–57145–152–8
    1. Cookery. India I. Title
TX724.5.I4H86   1998   98-7571
641.5954--dc21   CIP

Printed in Indonesia

2 3 4 5 6 99 00 01 02

Produced by Haldane Mason, London

Acknowledgments
Art Director: Ron Samuels
Editorial Director: Sydney Francis
Editorial Consultant: Christopher Fagg
Managing Editor: Jo-Anne Cox
Design: Digital Artworks Partnership Ltd
Photography: Iain Bagwell
Home Economist: Penny Stephens
Home Economist's Assistants: Nicky Deeley, Sarwat Jehan, Jean Stephens

Note
Unless otherwise stated, milk is assumed to be full fat, eggs are medium,
and pepper is freshly ground black pepper.

Traditional Indian cooking methods involve using a substantial amount of cooking oil.
The reader may prefer to reduce the amount of cooking oil used in some of these
recipes if following a special diet.

Contents

Introduction

The subcontinent of India and Pakistan covers some 1.5 million square miles and comprises very many different cultures and religions, of which the main groups are the Hindus and Muslims, within each of which are smaller sects, the Parsees, and the Christians. All of these have influenced the eating habits and tastes of the various ethnic communities throughout the subcontinent. The food eaten in the north, for example, differs considerably from that of the south. The people of the north, which is a wheat-growing area, prefer Indian breads, such as *chapatis* or *paratas,* as their staple, while rice, which is grown in many of the southern states, is preferred by the southerners.

Muslims are the meat-eating population of India, but for religious reasons they do not eat anything derived from the pig, which is considered unclean. Hindus, a vast majority of whom are vegetarians, are forbidden to eat beef, because the cow is considered a sacred animal.

Spices and herbs have been used to flavor food for thousands of years in the East, and India has for centuries been an important source of spices for Western nations. Yet it is only in the last twenty years or so that the majority of people in the West have become generally aware of our spicy cuisine. This may well be due in part to the great ease of communication and the fact that many people are now traveling to the Indian subcontinent where they have the opportunity to taste a variety of dishes. But most of all, it has been due to the proliferation of Indian restaurants in towns and cities throughout the world. The Indian communities that have settled in other countries have not only preserved their own culture and eating habits but, through the trade of special ingredients, have made real Indian cooking possible on a far wider scale.

Indian dishes are wonderfully good-tempered, in that very few of them need any last minute attention (maybe just sprinkling with a garnish in some cases). The majority of dishes can be made well in advance and will freeze successfully—and indeed, some actually improve through keeping. Others will usually keep in a refrigerator for a day or so until you are ready to reheat them; this means that the cook, provided the meal has been planned carefully, can join his or her guests for a pre-dinner drink without the slightest worry about what might be happening in the kitchen. Also, because it is perfectly correct to serve all the dishes, other than dessert, at once, there is no need to leap up from the first course in order to get the main course organized—everything can go on the table at the beginning of the meal.

What about the question of spiciness? Must you spend a fortune on a cupboard full of exotic items before you even begin? And how do you gauge what degree of "hotness" will be acceptable to your guests? Almost all the recipes in this book contain spices, but not necessarily a wide selection for each individual dish. Some curries, for example, require just two types of spice, another might need a combination of, say, twelve different herbs and spices. However, if you know you like Indian food and are likely to be cooking it on a regular basis, it is advisable to buy a basic range of spices for your own convenience (see Spices, opposite), which will see you through a good variety of recipes. Then build up gradually as you start to try others. Hotness often depends on the amount of chili, in whatever form: fresh chilies, which are used a great deal for garnish as well as in curry sauces, dried chilies, and ground chili (chili powder also known as cayenne pepper). It is advisable to under- rather than over-estimate the amount of chili you will need until you gain some experience in Indian cooking, and to remember that you can take some of the sting out of chili pods by scraping out the seeds. But, most importantly, do not make the mistake of thinking that all Indian curries must be red-hot to be authentic.

They need not be, and moreover usually a variety of mild and hot dishes are served at any given meal. You should always plan your meals to include both milder and hotter dishes because there is no point in destroying your guests' palates for your more delicately flavored dishes by killing their taste buds with chili.

EQUIPMENT FOR INDIAN COOKING

Your own kitchen will probably be equipped already with everything needed for cooking a full range of Indian dishes. Some good-quality saucepans, with thick bases, and a heavy-based skillet are essential, and you will want some wooden spatulas and, ideally, a slotted spoon for stirring rice, to use with them. Kitchen scales, although not essential, could be helpful, too.

For grinding spices you can use a pestle and mortar, a coffee grinder, food processor, or a rolling-pin: in many Indian households a flat, heavy grindstone and something like a rolling-pin (called a *mussal*) are still considered the best solution. Some people find a garlic press useful, too, for Indian cooking.

SPICES

Your basic stock of spices should include fresh ginger and garlic, chili powder, turmeric, cardamom, black pepper, ground coriander, and cumin. The powdered spices will keep very well in airtight containers, carefully labeled, while the fresh ginger and garlic will keep for 7–10 days in the refrigerator. Other useful items, to be acquired as your repertoire increases, are cumin seeds (black as well as white), onion seeds, mustard seeds, cloves, cinnamon, dried red chilies, fenugreek seeds, vegetable ghee, and garam masala (a mixture of spices that can either be bought ready-made or homemade in quantity for use whenever required). Tomato paste is also useful.

USING SPICES

There are many ways of using spices. You can use them whole, ground, toasted, fried, or mixed with yogurt to marinate meat and poultry. One spice can alter the flavor of a dish and a combination of several can produce different colors and textures.

The quantities of spices shown in the recipes in this book are merely a guide. Do not hesitate to increase or decrease them as you wish, especially in the cases of salt and chili powder, which are very much a matter of taste.

Many of the recipes in this book call for ground spices, which are generally available in supermarkets, as well as in Indian and Pakistani grocery stores. In India we almost always buy whole spices and grind them ourselves, and there is no doubt that freshly ground spices do make a noticeable difference to the taste. However, there is no denying that it is more convenient, and quicker, to use ground spices.

For some of the recipes in this book, the spices need to be roasted. In India this is done on a *thawa*, but you can use a heavy, ideally cast-iron skillet. No water or oil is added to the spices: they are simply briefly dry-fried whole while the skillet is shaken to keep them from burning.

Remember that slow cooking over a fairly low heat will improve the taste of the food, as it allows the spices to be absorbed. This is why re-heating the following day is no problem for most Indian food. Feel free to experiment: only you know how you want your food to taste.

Meat & Fish

There is a wide variety of meat recipes in this chapter, and in most cases the meat is lamb. Leg of lamb is much less fatty than shoulder, but if you like shoulder, combine it with an equal proportion of leg, which works very well. In some of the recipes beef (braising steak, for example) may be substituted for lamb, but if you do this you will need to allow a little extra cooking time.

In India, chicken is expensive and is therefore considered a special-occasion meat. A chicken dish is invariably served at every function. Indians always cook chicken skinned and cut into small pieces. If the chicken weighs about 3¼ pounds it should be cut into about 8 pieces, unless you are making tandoori chicken, when chicken quarters look a lot better and are more appropriate. Ask your local butcher to skin, cut, and bone the chicken for you if required.

India may not be thought of as a great fish-eating nation, but there are certain parts of it, notably Bengal and around the city of Karachi, where fish is very popular. Indeed, the staple diet of the Bengalis is fish and rice; they enjoy river fish from the Hooghli and also lobster and jumbo shrimp.

Hot Spicy Lamb in Sauce

This North Indian dish is traditionally served for a late breakfast or brunch. Ideally it should be cooked all night and served in the morning with nan bread, but it can be cooked the day before and reheated.

Serves 6–8

INGREDIENTS

$^3/_4$ cup oil
$2^1/_4$ pounds lean leg of lamb, cut into large pieces
1 tbsp ground garam masala
5 medium onions, chopped
$^2/_3$ cup unsweetened yogurt
2 tbsp tomato paste
2 tsp finely chopped fresh ginger root

2 tsp crushed garlic
$1^1/_2$ tsp salt
2 tsp chili powder
1 tbsp ground coriander
2 tsp ground nutmeg
$3^3/_4$ cups water
1 tbsp ground fennel seeds
1 tbsp paprika
1 tbsp *bhoonay chanay* or gram flour

3 bay leaves
1 tbsp all-purpose flour
nan breads or paratas, to serve

TO GARNISH:
2–3 fresh green chilies, chopped
fresh cilantro leaves, chopped

1 Heat the oil in a pan and add the meat and half the garam masala. Stir-fry the mixture for 7–10 minutes, until the meat is well coated. Using a slotted spoon, remove the meat and set aside.

2 Add the onions to the pan and sauté until golden brown. Return the meat to the pan, reduce the heat, and simmer, stirring occasionally.

3 In a separate bowl, mix the yogurt and tomato paste, ginger, garlic, salt, chili powder, ground coriander, nutmeg, and the rest of the garam masala. Pour this mixture over the meat and stir-fry, mixing the spices well into the meat, for 5–7 minutes.

4 Add half the water, then the fennel, paprika, and *bhoonay chanay* or gram flour. Add the remaining water and the bay leaves, lower the heat, cover, and cook for 1 hour, stirring.

5 Mix the flour in 2 tbsp of warm water and pour this mixture over the curry. Garnish with the chilies and the cilantro and cook until the meat is tender and the sauce thickens. Serve with nan bread (see page 178) or paratas (see page 174).

Tomatoes Cooked with Meat & Yogurt

This delicious tomato khorma *has a
semi-thick sauce. Serve freshly made chapatis (see page 180) with it.*

Serves 2–4

INGREDIENTS

1 tsp garam masala

1 tsp finely chopped fresh
  ginger root

1 tsp crushed garlic

2 black cardamoms

1 tsp chili powder

1/2 tsp black cumin seeds

2 x 1-inch cinnamon sticks

1 tsp salt

2/3 cup unsweetened yogurt

1 pound 2 ounces lean cubed lamb

2/3 cup oil

2 onions, sliced

2 1/2 cups water

2 firm tomatoes, cut into quarters

2 tbsp lemon juice

TO GARNISH:

fresh cilantro leaves, chopped

2 fresh green chilies, chopped

1 In a large mixing bowl, mix together the garam masala, ginger, garlic, cardamoms, chili powder, black cumin seeds, cinnamon sticks, salt, and the yogurt until well combined.

2 Add the meat to the yogurt and spice mixture and mix well to coat. Set aside.

3 Heat the oil in a large saucepan and fry the onions until golden brown.

4 Add the meat to the pan and stir-fry for about 5 minutes. Reduce the heat, add the water, cover the pan, and simmer for about 1 hour, stirring occasionally.

5 Add the tomatoes to the curry and sprinkle with the lemon juice. Simmer for a further 7–10 minutes.

6 Garnish the curry with the cilantro leaves and the green chilies, and serve hot.

COOK'S TIP

Khormas *are slowly braised dishes, many of which are the rich and spicy, Persian-inspired Mogul dishes served on special occasions. Yogurt is often featured, both as a marinade and as the cooking liquid. In a properly cooked* khorma, *prime, tender cuts of meat are used, and the small amount of cooking liquid is absorbed into the meat to produce a succulent result.*

Lamb with Onions & Dried Mango Powder

This dish originates from Hyderabad, in central southern India.

Serves 4

INGREDIENTS

4 medium onions
1¼ cups oil
1 tsp finely chopped fresh
   ginger root
1 tsp crushed garlic

1 tsp chili powder
1 pinch turmeric
1 tsp salt
3 fresh green chilies
1 pound leg of lamb, cubed

2½ cups water
1½ tsp *aamchoor* (dried mango
   powder)
fresh cilantro leaves

1 Using a sharp knife, finely chop 3 onions.

2 Heat ⅔ cup of the oil in a pan and fry the onions until golden brown. Reduce the heat and add the ginger, garlic, chili powder, turmeric, and salt to the pan. Stir-fry the mixture for about 5 minutes, then add 2 of the chilies.

3 Add the meat to the pan and stir-fry the mixture for a further 7 minutes.

4 Add the water to the pan, cover, and cook over a low heat for 35–45 minutes, stirring occasionally.

5 Meanwhile, slice the remaining onion. Heat the remaining oil in a pan and fry the onion until golden. Set aside.

6 Once the meat is tender, add the *aamchoor* (dried mango powder), the remaining green chili, and fresh cilantro leaves and stir-fry for 3–5 minutes.

7 Transfer the curry to a serving dish and pour the fried onion slices and oil along the center. Serve hot.

COOK'S TIP

Aamchoor *(dried mango powder) is made from dried raw mangoes. It has a sour taste and can be bought in jars.*

Lamb Pot Roast

This dish is great for dinner parties. Serve it with vegetable rice (see page 162) and potatoes with spices and onions (see page 108).

Serves 6

INGREDIENTS

5^1/$_2$ pounds leg of lamb
2 tsp finely chopped fresh
   ginger root
2 tsp fresh garlic, crushed
2 tsp garam masala
1 tsp salt

2 tsp black cumin seeds
4 black peppercorns
3 cloves
1 tsp chili powder
3 tbsp lemon juice
1^1/$_4$ cups oil

1 large onion, peeled
about 10 cups water

1 Remove the fat from the lamb. Prick the lamb all over with a fork.

2 In a bowl, mix the ginger, garlic, garam masala, salt, black cumin seeds, peppercorns, cloves, and chili powder until well combined. Stir in the lemon juice and mix well. Rub the mixture all over the leg of lamb and set aside.

3 Heat the oil in a pan. Add the meat to the pan and place the onion alongside the leg of lamb.

4 Add enough water to cover the meat and cook over a low heat for 2^1/$_2$–3 hours, turning occasionally. (If after awhile the water has evaporated and the meat is not tender, add a little extra water.) Once the water has completely evaporated, turn the roast over to brown it on all sides.

5 Remove the roast from the pan and transfer to a serving dish. Cut the roast into slices or serve it whole to be carved at the table. Serve hot or cold.

COOK'S TIP

Traditionally, a pan called a degchi is used for pot-roasting in India. It is set over hot ashes and contains hot coals in its lid.

Broiled Ground Lamb

This is a rather unusual way of cooking ground meat. In India this is cooked on a naked flame, but a broiler works just as well.

Serves 4

INGREDIENTS

5 tbsp oil
2 onions, sliced
1 pound ground lamb
2 tbsp unsweetened yogurt
1 tsp chili powder
1 tsp finely chopped fresh
   ginger root

1 tsp crushed garlic
1 tsp salt
$1^1/_2$ tsp garam masala
$^1/_2$ tsp ground allspice
2 fresh green chilies
fresh cilantro leaves

TO GARNISH:
1 onion, cut into rings
fresh cilantro leaves, chopped
1 lemon, cut into wedges

1 Heat the oil in a saucepan. Add the onions and sauté until golden brown.

2 Place the ground lamb in a large bowl. Add the yogurt, chili powder, ginger, garlic, salt, garam masala, and ground allspice and mix to combine.

3 Add the lamb mixture to the fried onions and stir-fry for 10–15 minutes. Remove from the heat and set aside.

4 Meanwhile, place the green chilies and half the cilantro leaves in a food processor and process. Alternatively, finely chop the green chilies and cilantro with a sharp knife. Set aside until required.

5 Put the ground lamb mixture in a food processor and process. Alternatively, place in a large bowl and mash with a fork. Mix the lamb mixture with the chilies and cilantro and blend well.

6 Transfer the mixture to a shallow flameproof dish. Cook under a preheated broiler for 10–15 minutes, moving the mixture about with a fork. Watch it carefully to prevent it from burning.

7 Serve garnished with onion rings, cilantro, and lemon wedges.

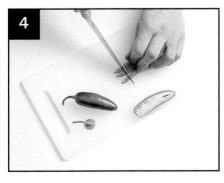

Ground Lamb with Peas

Served with a dhal *and rice, this simple dish makes a well-balanced meal.*

Serves 4

INGREDIENTS

1 medium onion
6 tbsp oil
3 fresh red chilies
fresh cilantro leaves

2 tomatoes, chopped
1 tsp salt
1 tsp finely chopped fresh
  ginger root
1 tsp crushed garlic

1 tsp chili powder
1 pound lean ground lamb
1 cup peas

1 Peel and slice the onion, using a sharp knife.

2 Heat the oil in a medium-size saucepan. Add the onion slices and sauté until golden brown.

3 Add 2 of the red chilies, half of the fresh cilantro leaves, and the chopped tomatoes to the pan and reduce the heat to a simmer.

4 Add the salt, ginger, garlic, and chili powder to the mixture in the pan and stir well to combine.

5 Add the ground lamb to the pan and stir-fry the mixture for 7–10 minutes.

6 Add the peas to the mixture in the pan and cook for a further 3–4 minutes, stirring occasionally.

7 Transfer the lamb and pea mixture to warm serving plates and garnish with the remaining red chili and the fresh cilantro leaves.

COOK'S TIP

The flavor of garlic can be changed according to how it is prepared. For instance, a whole garlic clove added to a dish will give it the flavor but not the "bite" of garlic; a halved clove will add a little bite, a finely chopped garlic clove will release most of the flavor, and a crushed clove will release all of the flavor.

Lamb Curry in a Thick Sauce

Originally a Kashmiri dish, this lamb stew is now made all over India and is popular wherever Indian food is eaten. Noted for its delicious tomato-flavored sauce, it is ideal for a dinner party.

Serves 6

INGREDIENTS

2¹/₄ pounds lean lamb, with or without bone

7 tbsp unsweetened yogurt

5 tbsp almonds

2 tsp garam masala

2 tsp finely chopped fresh ginger root

2 tsp crushed garlic

1¹/₂ tsp chili powder

1¹/₂ tsp salt

1¹/₄ cups oil

3 onions, finely chopped

4 green cardamoms

2 bay leaves

3 fresh green chilies, chopped

2 tbsp lemon juice

14 ounce can tomatoes

1¹/₄ cups water

fresh cilantro leaves, chopped

1 Using a very sharp knife, cut the lamb into small, even-size pieces.

2 In a large mixing bowl, combine the yogurt, almonds, garam masala, ginger, garlic, chili powder, and salt, stirring to mix well.

3 Heat the oil in a large saucepan and fry the onions with the cardamoms and the bay leaves, stirring constantly, until golden brown.

4 Add the meat and the yogurt mixture to the pan and stir-fry for 3–5 minutes.

5 Add 2 green chilies, the lemon juice, and the canned tomatoes to the mixture in the pan and stir-fry for a further 5 minutes.

6 Add the water to the pan, cover, and simmer over a low heat for 35–40 minutes.

7 Add the remaining green chili and the cilantro leaves and stir

until the sauce has thickened. (Remove the lid and turn the heat higher if the sauce is too watery.)

8 Transfer the curry to warm serving plates and serve hot.

Potatoes Cooked with Meat & Yogurt

Khormas almost always contain yogurt and therefore have lovely, smooth sauces. A good accompaniment would be chapatis (see page 180), or fried spicy rice (see page 160) with peas.

Serves 6

INGREDIENTS

3 medium onions
3 medium potatoes
1^1/$_4$ cups oil
2^1/$_4$ pounds leg of lamb, cubed with
   or without bone
2 tsp garam masala
1^1/$_2$ tsp finely chopped fresh
   ginger root

1^1/$_2$ tsp fresh garlic, crushed
1 tsp chili powder
3 black peppercorns
3 green cardamoms
1 tsp black cumin seeds
2 cinnamon sticks
1 tsp paprika
1^1/$_2$ tsp salt

^{2}/$_3$ cup unsweetened yogurt
2^1/$_2$ cups water

TO GARNISH:
2 fresh green chilies, chopped
fresh cilantro leaves, chopped

1 Peel and slice the onions and set aside. Peel and cut each potato into 6 pieces.

2 Heat the oil in a saucepan and fry the sliced onions until golden brown. Remove the onions from the pan and set aside.

3 Add the meat to the saucepan with 1 tsp of the garam masala and stir-fry for about 5–7 minutes over a low heat.

4 Add the onions to the pan and remove from the heat.

5 Meanwhile, in a small bowl, mix together the ginger, garlic, chili powder, peppercorns, cardamoms, cumin seeds, cinnamon sticks, paprika, and salt. Add the yogurt and mix well.

6 Return the pan to the heat and gradually add the spice and yogurt mixture to the meat

and onions and stir-fry for 7–10 minutes. Add the water, lower the heat, and cook, covered, for about 40 minutes, stirring the mixture occasionally.

7 Add the potatoes to the pan and cook, covered, for a further 15 minutes, gently stirring the mixture occasionally. Garnish with green chilies and fresh cilantro leaves, and serve at once.

Lean Lamb Cooked in Spinach

Serve this nutritious combination of lamb and spinach with plain boiled rice and tomato curry (see page 134).

Serves 2–4

INGREDIENTS

1¼ cups oil
2 medium onions, sliced
¼ bunch fresh cilantro
3 fresh green chilies, chopped
1½ tsp finely chopped fresh
  ginger root
1½ tsp crushed garlic
1 tsp chili powder

½ tsp turmeric
1 pound lean lamb, with or
  without the bone
1 tsp salt
2¼ pounds fresh spinach, trimmed,
  washed, and chopped or
  15 ounce can spinach
3¼ cups water

TO GARNISH:
fresh ginger root, peeled
  and shredded
fresh cilantro leaves

1 Heat the oil in a saucepan and fry the onions until they turn a pale color.

2 Add the fresh cilantro and 2 of the chopped green chilies to the pan and stir-fry for 3–5 minutes.

3 Reduce the heat and add the ginger, garlic, chili powder, and turmeric to the mixture in the pan, stirring to mix.

4 Add the lamb to the pan and stir-fry for a further 5 minutes. Add the salt and the fresh or canned spinach and cook, stirring occasionally with a wooden spoon, for a further 3–5 minutes.

5 Add the water, stirring, and cook over a low heat, covered, for about 45 minutes. Remove the lid and check the meat. If it is not tender, turn it over, increase the heat, and cook, uncovered, until the surplus water has been absorbed. Stir-fry the mixture for a further 5–7 minutes.

6 Transfer the lamb and spinach mixture to a serving dish and garnish with shredded ginger, fresh cilantro leaves, and the remaining chopped green chili. Serve hot.

Spicy Lamb Chops

This is an attractive way of serving lamb chops, especially if you garnish them with French fries, tomatoes, and lemon wedges. Serve these with any dhal *and rice or chapatis (see page 180).*

Serves 4–6

INGREDIENTS

2¼ pounds lamb chops
2 tsp finely chopped fresh
  ginger root
2 tsp crushed garlic
1 tsp pepper
1 tsp garam masala

1 tsp black cumin seeds
1½ tsp salt
3¾ cups water
2 medium eggs
1½ cups oil

TO GARNISH:
French fries
tomatoes
lemon wedges

1 Using a sharp knife, trim away any excess fat from the lamb chops.

2 Mix the ginger, garlic, pepper, garam masala, cumin seeds, and salt together and rub all over the chops.

3 Bring the water to a boil, add the chops and spice mixture, and cook for about 45 minutes, stirring occasionally. Once the water has evaporated, remove from the heat and set aside to cool.

4 Using a fork, beat the eggs together in a large bowl.

5 Heat the oil in a large saucepan.

6 Dip each lamb chop into the beaten egg and then fry them in the oil for 3 minutes, turning once.

7 Transfer the chops to a large serving dish and garnish with French fries, tomatoes, and lemon wedges. Serve hot.

COOK'S TIP

Garam masala is a mixture of ground spices, not an individual spice. The usual combination includes cardamom, cinnamon, cloves, cumin, nutmeg, and black peppercorns, but most Indian cooks have a personal recipe, often handed down for generations. You can buy prepared garam masala at large supermarkets or Asian grocery stores.

Stuffed Tomatoes

This is an impressive dinner-party dish—serve as an appetizer
You will find large tomatoes are easier to fill.

Serves 4–6

INGREDIENTS

6 large, firm tomatoes
4 tbsp sweet butter
1 medium onion, finely chopped
5 tbsp oil

1 tsp finely chopped fresh
  ginger root
1 tsp crushed garlic
1 tsp pepper
1 tsp salt

$^1/_2$ tsp garam masala
1 pound ground lamb
1 fresh green chili
fresh cilantro leaves

1 Preheat the oven to 350°F. Rinse the tomatoes, cut off the tops, and scoop out the flesh.

2 Grease a heatproof dish with 2 tbsp butter. Place the tomatoes in the dish.

3 Heat the oil in a pan and sauté the onion until golden.

4 Lower the heat and add the ginger, garlic, pepper, salt, and garam masala. Stir-fry the mixture for 3–5 minutes.

5 Add the ground lamb to the saucepan and fry for 10–15 minutes.

6 Add the green chili and fresh cilantro leaves and continue stir-frying the mixture for about 3–5 minutes.

7 Spoon the lamb mixture into the tomatoes and replace the tops. Cook the tomatoes in the oven for 15–20 minutes.

8 Transfer the tomatoes to serving plates and serve hot.

VARIATION

You could use the same recipe to stuff red or green bell peppers, if desired.

Cubed Lamb Kabobs

These kabobs taste even more delicious when they are barbecued out in the open air. In India, people sit out at night to watch as their kabobs are barbecued.

Serves 6–8

INGREDIENTS

2¼ pounds boneless, lean lamb, cubed

1 tsp meat tenderizer

1½ tsp finely chopped fresh ginger root

1½ tsp crushed garlic

1 tsp chili powder

½ tsp turmeric

½ tsp salt

2 tbsp water

8 tomatoes, cut in half

8 small pickling onions

10 mushrooms

1 green bell pepper, cut into large pieces

1 red bell pepper, cut into large pieces

2 tbsp oil

2 lemons, cut into quarters, to garnish

1 Wash the meat and place it in a dish. Apply the tenderizer to the meat, using your hands. Set aside for about 3 hours at room temperature.

2 Mix together the ginger, garlic, chili powder, turmeric, and salt in a bowl. Add the water and mix to form a paste. Add the meat and mix until it is well coated with the spices.

3 Arrange the meat cubes on skewers, alternating with the tomatoes, pickling onions, mushrooms, and bell peppers. Brush the meat and vegetables with the oil.

4 Broil the kabobs under a preheated broiler for 25–30 minutes, or until the meat is cooked through. When cooked, remove the kabobs from the broiler and transfer to a serving plate. Arrange lemon wedges on the side and serve immediately with boiled rice and a raita (see page 216).

COOK'S TIP

If using wooden skewers, soak them in cold water for 20 minutes before they are used to prevent them from burning during cooking.

Cauliflower with Meat

Vegetables with meat, especially cauliflower and spinach, have a lovely flavor cooked this way. This uses only a few spices, but baghaar *(seasoned oil dressing) is added at the end.*

Serves 4

INGREDIENTS

1 medium cauliflower
2 fresh green chilies
1 1/4 cups oil
2 onions, sliced
1 pound cubed lamb
1 1/2 tsp finely chopped fresh
   ginger root

1 1/2 tsp crushed garlic
1 tsp chili powder
1 tsp salt
fresh cilantro leaves, chopped
3 3/4 cups water
1 tbsp lemon juice

BAGHAAR:
2/3 cup oil
4 dried red chilies
1 tsp mixed mustard and
   onion seeds

1 Using a sharp knife, cut the cauliflower into small florets. Chop the green chilies.

2 Heat the oil in a large saucepan. Add the onions and fry until golden brown.

3 Reduce the heat and add the meat, stirring.

4 Add the ginger, garlic, chili powder, and salt. Stir-fry for about 5 minutes.

5 Add 1 green chili and half the cilantro leaves.

6 Stir in the water and cook, covered, over a low heat for about 30 minutes.

7 Add the cauliflower florets and simmer for a further 15–20 minutes, or until the water has evaporated completely. Stir-fry the mixture for another 5 minutes. Remove the pan from the heat and sprinkle the lemon juice sparingly.

8 To make the *baghaar*, heat the remaining oil in a separate small saucepan. Add the dried red chilies and the mixed mustard and onion seeds and fry until they turn a darker color, stirring occasionally. Remove the pan from the heat and pour the mixture over the cooked cauliflower.

9 Garnish with the remaining green chili and fresh cilantro leaves. Serve immediately.

Lamb & Lentils

This recipe uses four different types of lentils and dried oats. This takes some time as you have to cook the lamb khorma *separately. However, the result is truly delicious!*

Serves 6

INGREDIENTS

¹/₂ cup *chana dhal*
¹/₂ cup *masoor dhal*
1¹/₂ cup *moong dhal*
¹/₂ cup *urid dhal*
5 tbsp dried oats

KHORMA:
3 pound 5 ounces lamb, cubed,
 with bones
³/₄ cup unsweetened yogurt

2 tsp finely chopped fresh
 ginger root
2 tsp crushed garlic
1 tbsp garam masala
2 tsp chili powder
¹/₂ tsp turmeric
3 whole green cardamoms
2 cinnamon sticks
1 tsp black cumin seeds
2 tsp salt
2 cups oil

5 medium onions, sliced
3¹/₄ cups water
2 fresh green chilies
fresh cilantro leaves

TO GARNISH:
6 fresh green chilies, chopped
¹/₂ bunch fresh cilantro
 leaves, chopped
2 pieces fresh ginger root, shredded
3 lemons, cut into wedges

1 Soak the *dhals* and oats overnight. Boil in a pan of water until soft. Mash and set aside.

2 Place the lamb in a large bowl. Add the yogurt, spices and salt, mix and set aside.

3 Heat 1¹/₄ cups of the oil in a pan and fry 4 of the onions until golden. Add the meat and stir-fry for 7–10 minutes. Stir in the water, lower the heat, cover, and cook for 1 hour, stirring. If the meat is not tender, add more water and cook for a further 15–20 minutes. Remove from the heat.

4 Add the *dhals* to the meat, stir, and mix. If the mixture is too thick, add 1¹/₄ cups water, stir, and cook for 10–12 minutes. Add the chilies and the cilantro. Transfer to a serving dish and set aside.

5 Heat the remaining oil and fry the remaining onion until golden. Pour over the lamb and lentils. Garnish and serve immediately.

Meatballs in Sauce

*This is an old family recipe. The koftas (meatballs) are easy
to make and also freeze beautifully.*

Serves 4

INGREDIENTS

1 pound ground lamb
1 tsp fresh ginger root, crushed
1 tsp crushed garlic
1 tsp garam masala
1$\frac{1}{2}$ tsp poppy seeds
1 tsp salt
$\frac{1}{2}$ tsp chili powder
1 medium onion, finely chopped
1 fresh green chili, finely chopped
fresh cilantro leaves

1 tbsp gram flour
$\frac{2}{3}$ cup oil

SAUCE:
2 tbsp oil
3 medium onions, finely chopped
2 small cinnamon sticks
2 large black cardamoms
1 tsp finely chopped fresh
   ginger root

1 tsp crushed garlic
1 tsp salt
4$\frac{1}{2}$ tbsp unsweetened yogurt
$\frac{2}{3}$ cup water

TO GARNISH:
fresh cilantro leaves, finely chopped
1 fresh green chili, finely chopped

1 Place the lamb in a large mixing bowl.

2 Add the ginger, garlic, garam masala, poppy seeds, salt, chili powder, onion, chili, cilantro, and gram flour and mix well with a fork.

3 Make small meatballs out of the mixture with your hands and set aside.

4 To make the sauce, heat the oil and sauté the onions until golden brown. Add the cinnamon sticks and cardamoms to the pan, lower the heat, and stir-fry for a further 5 minutes. Add the ginger, garlic, salt, yogurt, and water and stir to mix well.

5 Transfer to a serving bowl and garnish with chopped cilantro and chilies.

6 Heat the oil and fry the meatballs, turning occasionally, for 8–10 minutes, or until golden.

7 Transfer the meatballs to warm serving plates. Serve with the sauce and chapatis (see page 180).

Shish Kabobs

These ground lamb kabobs should ideally be barbecued on skewers, but you may use the broiler—especially in the winter. They can be served as a starter or as part of a full-scale meal.

Makes 10–12

INGREDIENTS

meat tenderizer
1 pound lean ground lamb
fresh cilantro leaves
1 medium onion, finely chopped
2 fresh green chilies, finely chopped
2 tbsp unsweetened yogurt

1 tsp finely chopped fresh
   ginger root
1 tsp crushed garlic
1 tsp ground cumin
1 tsp ground coriander
1/2 tsp salt

1 tsp chili powder
1/2 tsp ground allspice
1 tsp garam masala
chili powder, to garnish
lemon wedges and raita, to serve

1 Apply the meat tenderizer to the ground lamb with your fingers and blend in well. Set aside for at least 3 hours.

2 Meanwhile, chop the cilantro finely. Mix the onion, fresh green chilies, and chopped cilantro in a bowl.

3 In a separate bowl, mix the yogurt with the ginger, garlic, ground cumin, ground coriander, salt, chili powder, ground allspice, and garam masala. Blend with the onion mixture.

4 Blend the combined mixture into the ground lamb and mix together with your hands. Divide the mixture into 10–12 equal portions. Roll each portion around a skewer with your fingers, gently pressing all around.

5 Broil the kabobs under a preheated broiler, basting with oil occasionally.

6 Sprinkle with chili powder and serve immediately with lemon wedges and a raita (see page 216).

VARIATION

These kabobs are delicious cooked over a barbecue. Serve in pita bread for great party food. The cooked meat can also be chopped into a salad.

Spicy Lamb Curry in Sauce

This curry is especially good served with plain boiled rice and onion dhal (see page 142).
Tamarind is traditionally used for this recipe, but lemon juice works just as well.

Serves 4

INGREDIENTS

2 tsp ground cumin
2 tsp ground coriander
2 tsp shredded coconut
1 tsp mixed mustard and onion seeds
2 tsp sesame seeds

1 tsp finely chopped fresh
   ginger root
1 tsp crushed garlic
1 tsp chili powder
1 tsp salt
1 pound lean lamb

2 cups oil
3 medium onions, sliced
3³/₄ cups water
2 tbsp lemon juice
4 fresh green chilies, split

1 Dry-fry the ground cumin, ground coriander, shredded coconut, mixed mustard and onion seeds, and the sesame seeds in a heavy skillet, shaking the pan frequently to keep the spices from burning and sticking to the bottom of the pan. Grind the fried spices using a pestle and mortar.

2 In a large mixing bowl, blend together the fried ground spices with the ginger, garlic, chili powder, salt, and the cubed lamb and set aside.

3 In a separate pan, heat 1¹/₂ cups of the oil and fry the onions until golden brown.

4 Add the meat mixture to the onions and stir-fry for 5–7 minutes over a low heat. Add the water and simmer for 45 minutes, stirring occasionally. When the meat is cooked through, remove from the heat and sprinkle with the lemon juice.

5 In a separate saucepan, heat the remaining oil and add the

four split green chilies. Reduce the heat and cover with a lid. Remove the pan from the heat after about 30 seconds and set aside to cool.

6 Pour the chili oil mixture over the meat curry and serve hot with onion dhal (see page 142) and plain boiled rice.

Meat-Coated Eggs

These are ideal for taking on a picnic, because they are dry.

Serves 6

INGREDIENTS

1 pound lean ground lamb
1 small onion, finely chopped
1 fresh green chili, finely chopped
1 tsp finely chopped fresh
   ginger root

1 tsp crushed garlic
1 tsp ground coriander
1 tsp garam masala
1 tsp salt

1^1/$_2$ tbsp gram flour
7 eggs, 6 of them hard-boiled and
   shelled, 1 beaten
oil, for deep-frying

1 Place the lamb, onion, and the green chili in a bowl and mix together. Transfer the mixture to a food processor and work until well ground. (Alternatively, grind by hand using a pestle and mortar).

2 Remove the mixture from the food processor and add the ginger, garlic, ground coriander, garam masala, salt, gram flour, and the beaten egg. Combine the mixture together with your hands.

3 Divide the mixture into 6 equal portions. Roll each portion out to form a flat patty, about 1/4 inch thick. Place a hard-boiled egg in the middle of each patty and wrap the meat mixture around the egg to enclose it completely. When all 6 eggs have been covered, set aside in a cool place for 20–30 minutes.

4 Meanwhile, heat the oil in a *karahi* or deep skillet. Gently drop the meat-coated eggs into the oil and fry for 2–4 minutes, or until golden brown. Using a slotted spoon, remove the meat-coated eggs from the oil, transfer to paper towels, drain, and serve.

VARIATION

If you wish to serve these meat-coated eggs in a sauce, use the recipe for meatballs in sauce (see page 36).

Pork & Mushroom Curry

Vary the meat used here according to personal taste, using lean leg or shoulder of lamb or braising beef instead of pork. Omit the finishing touches (see step 4), if desired.

Serves 4

INGREDIENTS

1 pound 10 ounces leg or shoulder of pork
3 tbsp vegetable oil
2 onions, sliced
2 garlic cloves, crushed
1-inch piece ginger root, finely chopped
2 fresh green chilies, seeded and chopped, or 1–2 tsp chili powder

$1^{1}/2$ tbsp medium curry paste
1 tsp ground coriander
6-9 ounces thickly sliced mushrooms
$3^{1}/2$ cups stock
3 tomatoes, chopped
$^{1}/2$–1 tsp salt
2 ounces creamed coconut, chopped
2 tbsp ground almonds

TO GARNISH:
2 tbsp vegetable oil
1 green or red bell pepper, seeded and cut into thin strips
6 scallions, trimmed and sliced
1 tsp cumin seeds

1 Cut the pork into small bite-size pieces. Heat the oil in a saucepan, add the pork, and fry until sealed, stirring frequently. Remove the pork from the pan.

2 Add the onions, garlic, ginger, chilies, curry paste, and coriander to the saucepan and cook gently for 2 minutes. Stir in the mushrooms, stock, and tomatoes, and season with a little salt to taste.

3 Return the pork to the pan, cover, and simmer very gently for $1^{1}/4$–$1^{1}/2$ hours, or until the pork is tender.

4 Stir the creamed coconut and ground almonds into the curry, then cover the pan, and cook gently for 3 minutes.

5 Meanwhile, make the garnish. Heat the oil in a skillet, add the bell pepper strips and scallion slices, and sauté gently until glistening and tender-crisp. Stir in the cumin seeds and sauté gently for 30 seconds. Spoon the mixture over the curry and serve at once.

COOK'S TIP

Creamed coconut is sold in compressed bars and gives a rich flavor and texture to dishes.

Beef Kabobs

This dish is best served with the fried spicy rice (see page 160) and a dhal or a wet vegetable curry.

Makes 10–12

INGREDIENTS

3 tbsp *chana dhal*
1 pound boneless, lean beef, cubed
1 tsp finely chopped fresh
   ginger root
1 tsp crushed garlic
1 tsp chili powder
1 1/2 tsp salt

1 1/2 tsp garam masala
3 fresh green chilies
fresh cilantro leaves
1 medium onion, chopped
1 1/4 cups oil
3 1/2 cups water
2 tbsp unsweetened yogurt

1 medium egg

TO GARNISH:
onion rings
fresh green chilies

1 Rinse the *chana dhal* twice, removing any stones or other impurities. Boil the *chana dhal* in a pan of water until the water dries up and the *chana dhal* has softened. Place in a food processor and mash to form a paste.

2 Thoroughly mix the meat, ginger, garlic, chili powder, salt, and garam masala in a bowl. Add 2 of the green chilies, half the fresh cilantro leaves, and the onion.

3 Heat 2 tbsp of the oil in a saucepan. Add the meat mixture to the pan. Add the water and cook, covered, over a low heat for 45–60 minutes. Once the meat is tender, eliminate any excess water by removing the lid and cooking for a further 10–15 minutes. Place the meat in a food processor and mash.

4 Place the yogurt, egg, mashed *chana dhal* paste, the remaining green chili, and the cilantro leaves in a bowl and mix together with your fingers. Break off small balls of the meat paste and make about 12 small, flat patties between the palms of your hands.

5 Heat the remaining oil in a skillet and cook the patties, in batches, turning once.

6 Garnish with onion rings and fresh green chilies and serve immediately.

Sliced Beef with Yogurt & Spices

There are many different ways of cooking this dish. However, you need to fry the spices, as this gives the dish a dark color and a richer taste. Serve with chapati and lentils.

Serves 4

INGREDIENTS

1 pound lean beef slices, cut into 1-inch slices
5 tbsp unsweetened yogurt
1 tsp finely chopped fresh ginger root
1 tsp crushed garlic
1 tsp chili powder
1 pinch turmeric

2 tsp garam masala
1 tsp salt
2 cardamoms
1 tsp black cumin seeds
$1/4$ cup ground almonds
1 tbsp shredded coconut
1 tbsp poppy seeds
1 tbsp sesame seeds

$1\frac{1}{4}$ cups oil
2 medium onions, finely chopped
$1\frac{1}{4}$ cups water
2 fresh green chilies
a few fresh cilantro leaves, chopped

1 Place the beef in a large bowl, mix with the yogurt, ginger, garlic, chili powder, turmeric, garam masala, salt, cardamoms, and black cumin seeds, and set aside until required.

2 Dry-fry the ground almonds, shredded coconut, poppy seeds, and sesame seeds in a heavy skillet until golden, shaking the skillet frequently to keep the spices from burning.

3 Work the spice mixture in a food processor until finely ground. (Add 1 tbsp of water to blend, if necessary.) Add the ground spice mixture to the meat mixture and combine.

4 Heat a little oil in a large saucepan and fry the onions until golden brown. Remove the onions from the pan. Stir-fry the meat in the remaining oil for about 5 minutes, then return the onions to the pan and stir-fry for a further 5–7 minutes. Add the water and simmer over a low heat, covered, for 25–30 minutes, stirring occasionally. Add the fresh green chilies and cilantro leaves and serve hot.

VARIATION

Substitute lamb for the beef in this recipe, if desired.

Beef Khorma with Almonds

*This khorma, a traditional northern Indian recipe,
has a thick sauce and is quite simple to cook.*

Serves 6

INGREDIENTS

1¼ cups oil
3 medium onions, finely chopped
2¼ pounds lean beef, cubed
1½ tsp garam masala
1½ tsp ground coriander
1½ tsp finely chopped fresh
   ginger root

1½ tsp crushed garlic
1 tsp salt
⅔ cup unsweetened yogurt
2 cloves
3 green cardamoms
4 black peppercorns
2½ cups water

TO GARNISH:
6 almonds, soaked, peeled
   and chopped
2 fresh green chilies, chopped
a few fresh cilantro leaves

1 Heat the oil in a saucepan. Add the onions and stir-fry until golden brown. Remove half the onions from the pan, set aside, and reserve.

2 Add the meat to the remaining onions in the pan and stir-fry for about 5 minutes. Remove the pan from the heat.

3 Mix the garam masala, ground coriander, ginger, garlic, salt, and yogurt in a bowl.

Gradually add the meat to the yogurt and spice mixture and mix to coat the meat on all sides. Place in the saucepan, return to the heat, and stir for 5–7 minutes, or until the mixture is nearly brown in color.

4 Add the cloves, green cardamoms, and black peppercorns. Add the water, lower the heat, cover, and simmer for about 45–60 minutes. If the water has completely evaporated but the

meat is still not tender enough, add another 1½ cups water and cook for a further 10–15 minutes, stirring occasionally.

5 Just before serving, garnish with the reserved onions, chopped almonds, green chilies, and the fresh cilantro leaves. Serve with chapatis (see page 180).

Beef Cooked in Whole Spices

This is a delicious way of cooking beef. The fragrant whole
spices perfectly complement the meat.

Serves 4

INGREDIENTS

1¹/₄ cups oil
3 medium onions, chopped finely
1-inch piece fresh ginger
   root, shredded
4 cloves garlic, shredded
2 cinnamon sticks

3 whole green cardamoms
3 whole cloves
4 whole black peppercorns
6 dried red chilies
²/₃ cup unsweetened yogurt

1 pound beef, cubed, with or without
   bone
3 fresh green chilies, chopped
2¹/₂ cups water
fresh cilantro leaves

---

1 Heat the oil in a skillet and fry the onion, stirring occasionally, until a golden brown color.

2 Reduce the heat and add the ginger, garlic, cinnamon sticks, green cardamoms, cloves, black peppercorns, and dried red chilies to the skillet and stir-fry for 5 minutes.

3 In a bowl, beat the yogurt with a fork. Add the yogurt to the fried onions and stir to combine.

4 Add the meat and 2 of the green chilies to the skillet and stir-fry for 5–7 minutes.

5 Gradually add the water to the skillet, stirring well. Cover and cook for 1 hour, stirring and adding more water if necessary.

6 When thoroughly cooked through, remove the skillet from the heat and transfer the beef and spice mixture to a serving dish. Garnish with the remaining chopped green chili and the fresh cilantro leaves.

VARIATION

Substitute lamb for the beef in this
recipe, if desired.

Fried Kidneys

*Fried lamb kidneys are a popular dish for a late breakfast or brunch,
served with paratas (see page 174) and fried eggs.*

Serves 4

INGREDIENTS

1 pound lamb's kidneys	1 tsp finely chopped fresh ginger	1/2 tsp salt
2 tsp turmeric	root	3 tbsp oil
1 green bell pepper, sliced	1 tsp crushed garlic	1 small onion, finely chopped
2/3 cup water	1 tsp chili powder	cilantro leaves, to garnish

1 Using a sharp knife, remove the very fine skin surrounding each kidney. Cut each kidney into 4–6 pieces.

2 Place the kidney pieces in a bowl of warm water with 2 teaspoons of turmeric and 2 teaspoons of salt for about 1 hour. Drain the kidneys thoroughly, then rinse them under cold running water until the water runs clear.

3 Place the kidneys in a small saucepan, together with the green bell pepper. Pour in enough water to cover and cook over a medium heat, leaving the lid of the pan slightly ajar so that the steam can escape, until all the water has evaporated.

4 Add the ginger, garlic, chili powder, and salt to the kidney mixture and blend until well combined.

5 Add the oil, onion, and cilantro to the pan, and stir-fry for 7–10 minutes.

6 Transfer the kidneys to a serving plate and serve hot.

COOK'S TIP

Many people are resistant to the idea of cooking or eating kidneys because they often have a rather strong smell—even when cooked. However, if you wash and soak them in water, you can largely avoid this problem.

Chicken Tikka

*For this very popular dish, small pieces of chicken are marinated
for a minimum of three hours in yogurt and spices.*

Serves 6

INGREDIENTS

1 tsp finely chopped fresh
  ginger root
1 tsp crushed garlic
1/2 tsp ground coriander
1/2 tsp ground cumin
1 tsp chili powder
3 tbsp unsweetened yogurt

1 tsp salt
2 tbsp lemon juice
a few drops of red food coloring
  (optional)
1 tbsp tomato paste
3 pounds 5 ounces chicken breast
1 onion, sliced

3 tbsp oil

TO GARNISH:
6 lettuce leaves
1 lemon, cut into wedges

1 Blend together the ginger, garlic, ground coriander, ground cumin, and chili powder in a large mixing bowl.

2 Add the yogurt, salt, lemon juice, red food coloring (if using), and the tomato paste to the spice mixture.

3 Using a sharp knife, cut the chicken into pieces. Add the chicken to the spice mixture and toss to coat thoroughly. Marinate in the refrigerator for at least 3 hours, preferably overnight.

4 Arrange the onion in the bottom of a heatproof dish. Carefully drizzle half the oil over the onion.

5 Arrange the marinated chicken pieces on top of the onion and cook under a preheated broiler, turning once and basting with the remaining oil, for 25–30 minutes.

6 Serve the chicken tikka on a bed of lettuce and garnish with the lemon wedges.

COOK'S TIP

Chicken Tikka can be served with nan breads (see page 178), raita (see page 216), and mango chutney (see page 218) or as an appetizer.

Chicken Tossed in Black Pepper

Using black pepper instead of chili powder produces a milder curry. This recipe is basically a stir-fry and can be prepared in a short time. The dish goes well with fried corn and peas.

Serves 4–6

INGREDIENTS

8 chicken thighs
1 tsp finely chopped fresh
  ginger root
1 tsp crushed garlic
1 tsp salt
1 1/2 tsp coarsely ground black pepper
2/3 cup oil

1 green bell pepper, roughly sliced
2/3 cup water
2 tbsp lemon juice

FRIED CORN & PEAS:
4 tbsp sweet butter
1 1/3 cups frozen corn kernels

2 cups frozen peas
1/2 tsp salt
1/2 tsp chili powder
1 tbsp lemon juice
fresh cilantro leaves,
  to garnish

1 Using a sharp knife, bone the chicken thighs, if desired.

2 Combine the ginger, garlic, salt, and black pepper together in a mixing bowl.

3 Add the chicken pieces to the black pepper mixture and set aside until required.

4 Heat the oil in a large pan. Add the chicken pieces and stir-fry for 10 minutes.

5 Reduce the heat and add the sliced green bell pepper and the water to the pan. Simmer for about 10 minutes, then sprinkle the 2 tablespoons of lemon juice into the pan.

6 Meanwhile, make the fried corn and peas. Melt the butter in a large skillet. Add the corn and peas and fry, stirring occasionally, for about 10 minutes. Add the salt and chili powder and fry for a further 5 minutes.

7 Sprinkle the lemon juice over the top and garnish with fresh cilantro leaves.

8 Transfer the chicken and bell pepper mixture to serving plates and serve with the fried corn and peas.

Chicken Kabobs

These kabobs are a deliciously different way of serving chicken.
Serve with any dhal *and chapatis (see page 180).*

Serves 6–8

INGREDIENTS

3 pounds 5 ounces boneless chicken
1/2 tsp ground cumin
4 cardamom seeds, crushed
1/2 tsp ground cinnamon
1 tsp salt
1 tsp finely chopped fresh
   ginger root

1 tsp crushed garlic
1/2 tsp ground allspice
1/2 tsp pepper
1 1/4 cups water
2 tbsp unsweetened yogurt
2 fresh green chilies

1 small onion
fresh cilantro leaves
1 medium egg, beaten
1 1/4 cups oil

1 Place the boned chicken in a large saucepan. Add the ground cumin, cardamom seeds, ground cinnamon, salt, ginger, garlic, ground allspice, and pepper and pour in the water. Bring the mixture to a boil until all the water has been absorbed.

2 Put the mixture in a food processor and process to form a smooth paste. Transfer the paste to a mixing bowl. Add the yogurt and blend together until well combined.

3 Place the green chilies, onion, and cilantro leaves in the food processor and process finely. Add to the chicken mixture and mix well. Add the beaten egg and mix to combine.

4 Break off 12–15 portions from the mixture and make small, flat patties between the palms of your hands.

5 Heat the oil in a saucepan and fry the patties gently, in batches, over a low heat, turning once. Drain thoroughly on paper towels and serve hot.

COOK'S TIP

Indian kabob dishes are not necessarily cooked on a skewer; they can also be served in a dish and are always dry dishes with no sauce.

Chicken & Onions

This dish represents one of the rare occasions yogurt is not used to cook chicken.
It has a lovely flavor and is perfect served with pulao rice (see page 158). It also freezes very well.

Serves 4

INGREDIENTS

1¼ cups oil
4 medium onions, finely chopped
1½ tsp finely chopped fresh
   ginger root
1½ tsp garam masala
1½ tsp crushed garlic

1 tsp chili powder
1 tsp ground coriander
3 whole cardamoms
3 peppercorns
3 tbsp tomato paste
8 skinless chicken thighs

1¼ cups water
2 tbsp lemon juice
1 fresh green chili
fresh cilantro leaves
green chili strips, to garnish

1 Heat the oil in a large skillet. Add the onion and fry, stirring occasionally, until golden brown.

2 Reduce the heat and add the ginger, garam masala, garlic, chili powder, ground coriander, whole cardamoms, and the peppercorns, stirring occasionally to mix.

3 Add the tomato paste to the mixture in the skillet and stir-fry for 5–7 minutes.

4 Add the chicken thighs to the pan and toss to coat with the spice mixture.

5 Pour the water into the saucepan, cover, and simmer for 20–25 minutes.

6 Add the lemon juice, green chili, and cilantro to the mixture, and combine.

7 Transfer the chicken and onions to serving plates, garnish, and serve hot.

COOK'S TIP

A dish of meat cooked with plenty of onions is called a do pyaza. This curry definitely improves if made in advance and then reheated before serving. This develops the flavors and makes them richer.

Chicken Drumsticks Deep-Fried with Herbs & Spices

This dish is very attractive and great for dinner parties. It should ideally be cooked and served from a karahi, *but if you do not have one, a deep, heavy skillet will do.*

Serves 4

INGREDIENTS

8 chicken drumsticks
1$^1/_2$ tsp finely chopped fresh ginger root
1$^1/_2$ tsp crushed garlic
1 tsp salt

2 medium onions, chopped
$^1/_2$ large bunch fresh cilantro leaves
4–6 fresh green chilies
2$^1/_2$ cups oil
4 firm tomatoes, cut into wedges

2 large green bell peppers, roughly chopped

1 Make 2–3 slashes in each piece of chicken. Rub the ginger, garlic, and salt over the chicken pieces and set aside.

2 Place half the onions, the cilantro leaves, and green chilies in a mortar and grind to a paste with a pestle. Rub the paste over the chicken pieces.

3 Heat the oil in a *karahi* or large skillet. Add the remaining onions and fry until golden brown. Remove the onions from the skillet with a slotted spoon and set aside.

4 Reduce the heat to medium and fry the chicken pieces, in batches of about 2 at a time, until cooked through (about 5–7 minutes per piece).

5 When all the chicken pieces are cooked through, remove them from the skillet, set aside, and keep warm.

6 Add the tomatoes and the bell peppers to the pan and cook them until they are softened but still have "bite."

7 Transfer the tomatoes and bell peppers to a serving plate and arrange the chicken pieces on top. Garnish with the reserved fried onions and serve.

Chicken Khorma

Chicken khorma *is one of the most popular curries,
and this one is perfect for a dinner party.*

Serves 4–6

INGREDIENTS

1¹/₂ tsp finely chopped fresh
   ginger root
1¹/₂ tsp crushed garlic
2 tsp garam masala
1 tsp chili powder
1 tsp salt
1 tsp black cumin seeds

3 green cardamoms, with husks
   removed and seeds crushed
1 tsp ground coriander
1 tsp ground almonds
²/₃ cup unsweetened yogurt
8 whole skinless chicken breasts
1¹/₄ cups oil

2 medium onions, sliced
²/₃ cup water
fresh cilantro leaves
fresh green chilies, chopped
boiled rice, to serve

1 Mix the ginger, garlic, garam masala, chili powder, salt, black cumin seeds, green cardamoms, ground coriander, and almonds with the yogurt.

2 Spoon the yogurt and spice mixture over the chicken breasts and set aside to marinate.

3 Heat the oil in a large skillet. Add the onions to the skillet and fry until golden brown in color.

4 Add the chicken breasts to the skillet, stir-frying for 5–7 minutes.

5 Add the water, cover, and simmer for 20–25 minutes.

6 Add the cilantro and green chilies and cook for a further 10 minutes, stirring gently from time to time.

7 Transfer to a serving plate and serve with boiled rice.

VARIATION

Chicken portions may be used instead of breasts, if preferred, and should be cooked for 10 minutes longer in step 5.

Buttered Chicken

*A simple and mouth-watering dish with a lovely thick sauce,
this makes an impressive centerpiece for a dinner party.*

Serves 4–6

INGREDIENTS

7 tbsp sweet butter
1 tbsp oil
2 medium onions, finely chopped
1 tsp finely chopped fresh
  ginger root
2 tsp garam masala
2 tsp ground coriander
1 tsp chili powder

1 tsp black cumin seeds
1 tsp crushed garlic
1 tsp salt
3 whole green cardamoms
3 whole black peppercorns
$^2/_3$ cup unsweetened yogurt
2 tbsp tomato paste
8 skinless chicken pieces

$^2/_3$ cup water
2 whole bay leaves
$^2/_3$ cup light cream

TO GARNISH:
fresh cilantro leaves
2 fresh green chilies, chopped

1 Heat the butter and oil in a large skillet. Add the onions and sauté until golden brown, stirring. Reduce the heat.

2 Crush the fresh ginger and place in a bowl. Add the garam masala, ground coriander, ginger, chili powder, black cumin seeds, garlic, salt, cardamoms, and black peppercorns and blend. Add the yogurt and tomato paste and stir to combine.

3 Add the chicken pieces to the yogurt and spice mixture and mix to coat well.

4 Add the chicken to the onions in the skillet and stir-fry vigorously, making semi-circular movements, for 5–7 minutes.

5 Add the water and the bay leaves to the mixture in the skillet and simmer for 30 minutes, stirring occasionally.

6 Add the cream and cook for a further 10–15 minutes.

7 Garnish with fresh cilantro leaves and green chilies and serve hot.

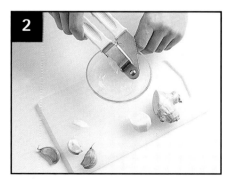

Tandoori-Style Chicken

In India, tandoori chicken is traditionally cooked in a tandoor (clay) oven. Alternatively, preheat the broiler to a very high temperature then lower it to medium to cook this dish.

Serves 4

INGREDIENTS

8 chicken drumsticks, skinned
$^2/_3$ cup natural yogurt
$1^1/_2$ tsp finely chopped fresh
  ginger root
$1^1/_2$ tsp crushed garlic
1 tsp chili powder
2 tsp ground cumin

2 tsp ground coriander
1 tsp salt
$^1/_2$ tsp red food coloring
1 tbsp tamarind paste
$^2/_3$ cup water
$^2/_3$ cup oil
lettuce leaves, to serve

TO GARNISH:
onion rings
sliced tomatoes
lemon wedges

1 Make 2–3 slashes in each piece of chicken.

2 Place the yogurt in a bowl. Add the ginger, garlic, chili powder, ground cumin, ground coriander, salt, and red food coloring and blend together until well combined.

3 Add the chicken to the yogurt and spice mixture and mix to coat well. Marinate the chicken in the refrigerator for a minimum of 3 hours.

4 In a separate bowl, mix the tamarind paste with the water and fold into the yogurt and spice mixture. Toss the chicken pieces in this mixture and set aside to marinate for a further 3 hours.

5 Transfer the chicken pieces to a heatproof dish and brush the chicken with a little of the oil. Cook the chicken under a preheated broiler for 30–35 minutes, turning the chicken pieces occasionally and basting with the remaining oil.

6 Arrange the chicken on a bed of lettuce and garnish with onion rings, sliced tomatoes, and lemon wedges.

COOK'S TIP

Prepare this dish ahead of time as the chicken is marinated for several hours. Nan bread (see page 178) and mint raita (see page 216) complement the dish perfectly.

Spicy Roast Chicken

This chicken dish, ideal for dinner parties, is cooked in the oven—which is very rare in Indian cooking. The chicken can be boned, if desired.

Serves 4

INGREDIENTS

¹/₄ cup ground almonds
¹/₃ cup shredded coconut
²/₃ cup oil
1 medium onion, finely chopped
1 tsp chopped fresh ginger root
1 tsp crushed garlic

1 tsp chili powder
1¹/₂ tsp garam masala
1 tsp salt
²/₃ cup yogurt
4 skinless chicken quarters
salad greens, to serve

TO GARNISH:
fresh cilantro leaves
1 lemon, cut into wedges

1 In a heavy-based saucepan, dry-fry the ground almonds and coconut and set aside.

2 Heat the oil in a skillet and fry the onion, stirring, until golden brown.

3 Place the ginger, garlic, chili powder, garam masala, and salt in a bowl and mix with the yogurt. Add the almonds and coconut and mix well.

4 Add the onions to the spice mixture, blend, and set aside.

5 Arrange the chicken quarters in the bottom of an ovenproof dish. Spoon the onion and spice mixture over the chicken sparingly.

6 Cook in a preheated oven at 425°F for 35–45 minutes. Check that the chicken is cooked thoroughly by piercing the thickest part of the meat with a sharp knife—the juices will run clear when the chicken is cooked through. Garnish with the cilantro and lemon wedges and serve with salad greens.

COOK'S TIP

If you want a spicier dish, add more chili powder and garam masala.

Chicken Jalfrezi

This is a quick and tasty way to use leftover roast chicken. The sauce can also be used for any cooked poultry, lamb, or beef.

Serves 4

INGREDIENTS

1 tsp mustard oil
3 tbsp vegetable oil
1 large onion, chopped finely
3 garlic cloves, crushed
1 tbsp tomato paste
2 tomatoes, peeled and chopped
1 tsp ground turmeric

$1/2$ tsp cumin seeds, ground
$1/2$ tsp coriander seeds, ground
$1/2$ tsp chili powder
$1/2$ tsp garam masala
1 tsp red wine vinegar
1 small red bell pepper, chopped

1 cup frozen fava beans
1 pound cooked chicken breasts, cut into bite-size pieces
salt
fresh cilantro sprigs, to garnish

1 Heat the mustard oil in a large skillet set over a high heat for about 1 minute, until it begins to smoke. Add the vegetable oil, reduce the heat, and add the onion and the garlic. Sauté the garlic and onion until they are golden.

2 Add the tomato paste, chopped tomatoes, ground turmeric, ground cumin, ground coriander seeds, chili powder, garam masala, and red wine vinegar to the skillet. Stir the mixture until fragrant.

3 Add the red bell pepper and fava beans and stir for 2 minutes, until the bell pepper is softened. Stir in the chicken, and salt to taste. Simmer gently for 6–8 minutes, until the chicken is heated through and the beans are tender.

4 Serve garnished with fresh cilantro leaves.

COOK'S TIP

This dish is an ideal way of making use of leftover poultry— turkey, duck, or quail. Any variety of beans works well, but vegetables are just as useful, especially root vegetables, zucchini, potatoes, or broccoli. Leafy vegetables will not be so successful.

Fried Fish in Gram Flour

*Very simple to make, this fried fish dish goes very well
with tomato curry (see page 134) and fried spicy rice (see page 160).*

Serves 4–6

INGREDIENTS

³/₄ cup gram flour
1 tsp finely chopped fresh
   ginger root
1 tsp crushed garlic
2 tsp chili powder
1 tsp salt

¹/₂ tsp turmeric
2 fresh green chilies, chopped
fresh cilantro leaves, chopped
1¹/₄ cups water
2¹/₄ pounds cod fillet
1¹/₄ cups oil

cooked rice, to serve

TO GARNISH:
2 lemons, cut into wedges
6 fresh green chilies, slit down
   the middle

1 Place the gram flour in a large mixing bowl. Add the ginger, garlic, chili powder, salt, and turmeric and mix to blend well.

2 Add the fresh green chilies and the cilantro leaves to the spiced mixture and stir to mix well.

3 Pour in the water and stir to form a semi-thick batter. Set aside until required.

4 Using a sharp knife, cut the cod into about 8 pieces.

5 Carefully dip the pieces of cod into the batter, coating the cod all over. Shake off any excess batter.

6 Heat the oil in a heavy-based skillet. Add the battered cod and fry, in batches, over a medium heat, turning once, until cooked through and golden.

7 Transfer the cod to a serving dish and garnish with the lemon wedges and green chilies. Serve the cod with cooked rice.

COOK'S TIP

Gram flour or chana dhal flour (lentil flour) is used to make pakoras (see page 192) and is also used to bind kabobs and other items. A combination of gram flour and ordinary whole-wheat flour makes a delicious Indian bread (see page 176).

Bengali-Style Fish

*Fresh fish is eaten a great deal in Bengal (Bangladesh), and this dish
is made with mustard oil which gives the fish a good flavor.*

Serves 4–6

INGREDIENTS

1 tsp turmeric
1 tsp salt
2¼ pounds cod fillet, skinned and
   cut into pieces
6 tbsp corn oil

4 fresh green chilies
1 tsp finely chopped fresh
   ginger root
1 tsp crushed garlic
2 medium onions, finely chopped

2 tomatoes, finely chopped
6 tbsp mustard oil
2 cups water
fresh cilantro leaves, chopped,
   to garnish

1 Mix together the turmeric and salt in a small bowl.

2 Spoon the turmeric and salt mixture over the fish pieces.

3 Heat the oil in a skillet. Add the fish to the skillet and fry until pale golden yellow. Remove the fish with a slotted spoon and set aside.

4 Place the green chilies, ginger, garlic, onions, tomatoes, and mustard oil in a mortar and grind with a pestle to form a paste. Alternatively, grind the ingredients in a food processor.

5 Transfer the spice paste to a saucepan and dry-fry until golden brown.

6 Remove the pan from the heat and gently place the fish pieces into the paste without breaking the fish up.

7 Return the pan to the heat, add the water, and cook the fish, uncovered, over a medium heat for 15–20 minutes.

8 Serve immediately, garnished with chopped cilantro.

COOK'S TIP

*In the hot and humid eastern plains
that surround Bengal, the mustard
plant flourishes, providing oil for
cooking and spicy seeds for
flavoring. Fish and seafood appear
in many meals, often flavored with
mustard oil.*

Shrimp with Bell Peppers

This is a colorful and impressive side dish for a dinner party. As there are not many spices in this recipe it is good to use a lot of fresh cilantro in it.

Serves 4

INGREDIENTS

1 pound frozen shrimp
¹/₂ bunch fresh cilantro leaves

1 tsp crushed garlic
1 tsp salt
1 medium green bell pepper, sliced

1 medium red bell pepper
6 tbsp sweet butter

1 Defrost the shrimp and rinse under cold running water twice. Drain the shrimp thoroughly and place in a large mixing bowl.

2 Using a sharp knife, finely chop the bunch of fresh cilantro.

3 Add the garlic, salt, and fresh cilantro leaves to the shrimp and set aside until required.

4 Core and seed the bell peppers and cut the flesh into thin slices, using a sharp knife.

5 Melt the butter in a large skillet. Add the shrimp to the pan and stir-fry, stirring and tossing the shrimp gently, for 10–12 minutes.

6 Add the bell peppers to the pan and cook for a further 3–5 minutes, stirring occasionally.

7 Transfer the shrimp and bell pepper to a serving dish and serve hot.

VARIATION

You could use large jumbo shrimp in this dish, if desired.

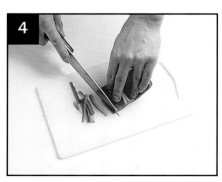

Shrimp with Spinach

This is an attractive dish to serve as an accompaniment, especially at parties, and will also freeze well.

Serves 4–6

INGREDIENTS

8 ounces frozen shrimp
12 ounces canned spinach purée
  or frozen spinach, thawed
  and chopped

2 tomatoes
$^2/_3$ cup oil
$^1/_2$ tsp mustard seeds
$^1/_2$ tsp onion seeds

1 tsp finely chopped fresh
  ginger root
1 tsp crushed garlic
1 tsp chili powder
1 tsp salt

1 Place the shrimp in a bowl of cold water and set aside to thaw thoroughly.

2 Drain the can of spinach purée, if using.

3 Using a sharp knife, cut the tomatoes into slices.

4 Heat the oil in a large skillet. Add the mustard and onion seeds to the pan.

5 Reduce the heat and add the tomatoes, spinach, ginger, garlic, chili powder, and salt to the skillet and stir-fry for about 5–7 minutes.

6 Drain the shrimp thoroughly and then pat dry with paper towels.

7 Add the shrimp to the spinach mixture in the skillet. Gently stir the shrimp and spinach mixture until well combined, cover, and simmer over a low heat for about 7–10 minutes.

8 Transfer the shrimp and spinach to a serving dish and serve hot.

COOK'S TIP

If using frozen spinach, it should be thawed and squeezed dry before using. You could use fresh spinach, if desired.

Tandoori-style Shrimp

These mouth-watering shrimp can be served as an appetizer arranged on a bed of lettuce with a lemon wedge, or as an attractive side dish for almost any meal.

Serves 4

INGREDIENTS

10–12 jumbo shrimp
8 tbsp sweet butter
1 tsp finely chopped fresh
   ginger root
1 tsp crushed garlic
1 tsp chili powder

¹/₂ tsp salt
1 tsp ground coriander
1 tsp ground cumin
fresh cilantro leaves, finely chopped
a few drops of red food coloring

TO GARNISH:
8 lettuce leaves
1–2 fresh green chilies,
   finely chopped
1 lemon, cut into wedges

1 Carefully remove the shells from the shrimp.

2 Transfer the shelled shrimp to a heatproof dish.

3 Melt the butter in a large saucepan.

4 Add the ginger, garlic, chili powder, salt, ground coriander, ground cumin, fresh cilantro leaves, and the red food coloring to the butter and mix together until thoroughly combined.

5 Brush the melted butter and spice mixture over the shrimp.

6 Cook the shrimp under a preheated broiler for 10–12 minutes, turning once.

7 Serve the shrimp on a bed of lettuce and garnish with finely chopped fresh green chilies and lemon wedges.

COOK'S TIP

Though not essential, it is best to shell the shrimp before cooking them as some people find it a bit awkward to shell them at the table.

Dried Shrimp

This is a more economical way of cooking shrimp. You can buy the
dried shrimp in packets from most Asian grocery stores

Serves 4

INGREDIENTS

7 ounces dried shrimp
1¼ cups oil
2 medium onions, sliced
3 fresh green chilies, finely chopped
fresh cilantro leaves, finely chopped

1½ tsp finely chopped fresh
 ginger root
1½ tsp crushed garlic
pinch of turmeric
1 tsp salt

1 tsp chili powder, plus extra
 to garnish
2 tbsp lemon juice

1 Soak the shrimp in a bowl of cold water for about 2 hours. Drain the shrimp thoroughly and rinse under cold running water twice. **Drain the shrimp again thoroughly.**

2 Heat ⅔ cup of the oil in a large saucepan.

3 Add the sliced onions, 2 of the fresh green chilies, and half the chopped fresh cilantro leaves to the saucepan and stir-fry until the onions are golden brown.

4 Add the ginger, garlic, turmeric, salt, chili powder, and lemon juice to the pan and stir-fry for a further 2 minutes over a low heat. Set aside until required.

5 Heat the remaining oil in a separate saucepan. Add the shrimp and fry, stirring occasionally, until the shrimp are crisp.

6 Add the fried shrimp to the onions and mix thoroughly together. Return the shrimp

and onion mixture to the heat and stir-fry for a further 3–5 minutes.

7 Transfer the shrimp to a serving dish, garnish with a pinch of chili powder, and serve with chapatis (see page 180).

VARIATION

You could use 1 pound fresh shrimp
instead of the dried shrimp,
if desired.

Shrimp with Tomatoes

Quick and easy to prepare, this dish is also extremely good to eat. Use the larger jumbo shrimp for special occasions, if desired.

Serves 4–6

INGREDIENTS

3 medium onions

1 green bell pepper

1 tsp finely chopped fresh
   ginger root

1 tsp crushed garlic

1 tsp salt

1 tsp chili powder

2 tbsp lemon juice

12 ounces frozen shrimp

3 tbsp oil

14 ounce can tomatoes

fresh cilantro leaves,
   to garnish

1 Using a sharp knife, slice the onions and the green bell pepper.

2 Place the ginger, garlic, salt, and chili powder in a small bowl and mix to combine. Add the lemon juice and mix to form a paste.

3 Place the shrimp in a bowl of cold water and set aside to thaw. Drain thoroughly.

4 Heat the oil in a medium-size saucepan. Add the onions and sauté until golden brown.

5 Add the spice paste to the onions, reduce the heat to low, and cook, stirring and mixing well, for about 3 minutes.

6 Add the tomatoes, tomato juice, and the green bell pepper, and cook for 5–7 minutes, stirring occasionally.

7 Add the shrimp to the pan and cook for 10 minutes, stirring occasionally.

8 Garnish with fresh cilantro leaves and serve hot with boiled rice and crisp salad greens.

COOK'S TIP

Fresh ginger root looks rather like a knobby potato. The skin should be peeled, then the flesh grated, finely chopped, or sliced. Ginger is also available ground: this can be used as a substitute for fresh ginger root, but the fresh root is far superior.

Vegetables

A great many people in India are vegetarians—possibly the majority. The reason for this is mainly religious, so over the years Indians have used their imaginations to create a vast range of different vegetarian dishes. Spinach, tomatoes, potatoes, green beans, and cauliflower are all commonly used in Indian cooking, but some popular Indian vegetables, including eggplant, okra, and white radish, are less familiar in the West despite the fact that they are now widely available. This chapter includes some simple but delicious vegetarian dishes using these vegetables— some in a sauce, some dry—that will help you to familiarize yourself with them.

In strict vegetarian households, neither fish nor even eggs are ever included in the diet, which means it lacks protein (and certain vitamins). That is why it is important to serve a dhal (lentils) as part of a vegetarian meal—all lentils are packed with protein. A raita (see page 216) makes an excellent accompaniment to any vegetarian meal, and for carbohydrates a good choice is plain boiled rice or pooris (see page 184).

Green Bean & Potato Curry

You can use fresh or canned green beans for this semi-dry vegetable curry. Serve an oil-dressed dhal (see page 144) with this, for a good contrast of flavors and colors.

Serves 4

INGREDIENTS

1¼ cups oil
1 tsp white cumin seeds
1 tsp mustard and onion seeds
4 dried red chilies
3 fresh tomatoes, sliced

1 tsp salt
1 tsp finely chopped fresh
  ginger root
1 tsp crushed garlic
1 tsp chili powder

7 ounces cut green beans
2 medium potatoes, peeled and diced
1¼ cups water
fresh cilantro leaves, chopped
2 green chilies, finely chopped

1 Heat the oil in a large, heavy-based saucepan.

2 Add the white cumin seeds, mustard and onion seeds, and dried red chilies to the saucepan, stirring well.

3 Add the tomatoes to the pan and stir-fry the mixture for 3–5 minutes.

4 Mix together the salt, ginger, garlic, and chili powder and spoon into the pan. Blend the whole mixture together.

5 Add the green beans and potatoes to the pan and stir-fry for about 5 minutes.

6 Add the water to the pan, reduce the heat, and simmer for 10–15 minutes, stirring occasionally.

7 Garnish the green bean and potato curry with chopped cilantro leaves and green chilies, and serve hot with cooked rice.

COOK'S TIP

Mustard seeds are often fried in oil or ghee to bring out their flavor before being combined with other ingredients.

Fried Cauliflower

A dry dish flavored with a few herbs, this is a very versatile accompaniment.

Serves 4

INGREDIENTS

4 tbsp oil
$^1/_2$ tsp onion seeds
$^1/_2$ tsp mustard seeds
$^1/_2$ tsp fenugreek seeds

4 dried red chilies
1 small cauliflower, cut into
   small florets
1 tsp salt

1 green bell pepper, diced

1 Heat the oil in a large, heavy-based saucepan.

2 Add the onion seeds, mustard seeds, fenugreek seeds, and the dried red chilies to the pan, stirring to mix.

3 Reduce the heat and gradually add all the cauliflower and the salt to the pan. Stir-fry the mixture for 7–10 minutes, coating the cauliflower in the spice mixture.

4 Add the diced green bell pepper to the pan and stir-fry the mixture for 3–5 minutes.

5 Transfer the spicy fried cauliflower to a serving dish and serve hot.

VARIATION

For a weekend feast or a special occasion, this dish looks great made with baby cauliflowers instead of florets. Baby vegetables are more widely available now, and the baby cauliflowers look very appealing on the plate. Peel off most of the outer leaves, leaving a few for decoration. Blanch the baby cauliflowers whole for 4 minutes and continue from step 3.

COOK'S TIP

Onion seeds are small and black. They may be labeled as kalonj *in Asian grocery stores. Onion seeds can be used instead of pepper, but have a spicier and more bitter taste.*

Eggplants & Yogurt

This is an unusual dish, in that the eggplant is first baked in the oven, then cooked in a saucepan.

Serves 4

INGREDIENTS

2 medium eggplants
4 tbsp oil
1 medium onion, sliced

1 tsp white cumin seeds
1 tsp chili powder
1 tsp salt

3 tbsp unsweetened yogurt
$^1/_2$ tsp mint sauce
fresh mint leaves, to garnish

1 Rinse the eggplants and pat dry with paper towels.

2 Arrange the eggplants in a single layer in an ovenproof dish. Bake in a preheated oven at 425°F for 45 minutes. Remove the baked eggplants from the oven and cool.

3 Cut the eggplants in half and, using a spoon, scoop out the eggplant flesh and reserve.

4 Heat the oil in a heavy-based saucepan. Add the onions and cumin seeds and fry, stirring, for 1–2 minutes.

5 Add the chili powder, salt, yogurt, and the mint sauce to the pan and stir well to mix.

6 Add the eggplant to the onion and yogurt mixture and stir-fry for 5–7 minutes or until all the liquid has been absorbed and the mixture is quite dry.

7 Transfer the eggplant and yogurt mixture to a serving dish, garnish with fresh mint leaves, and serve immediately.

COOK'S TIP

Rich in protein and calcium, yogurt plays an important part in Indian cooking. Thick unsweetened yogurt most closely resembles the yogurt made in many Indian homes.

Vegetable Kabobs

If you invite several people to dinner or to a buffet meal there is a strong chance that one of them may be a vegetarian. These kabobs are easy to make and taste delicious.

Makes 10–12

INGREDIENTS

2 large potatoes, sliced
1 medium onion, sliced
1/2 medium cauliflower, cut into
   small florets
1/2 cup peas
1 tbsp spinach paste

2–3 fresh green chilies
fresh cilantro leaves
1 tsp finely chopped fresh
   ginger root
1 tsp crushed garlic
1 tsp ground coriander

1 pinch turmeric
1 tsp salt
1 cup bread crumbs
1 1/4 cups oil
fresh chili strips, to garnish

1 Place the potatoes, onion, and cauliflower in a pan of water and bring to a boil. Reduce the heat and simmer until the potatoes are cooked through. Remove the vegetables from the pan with a slotted spoon and drain thoroughly.

2 Add the peas and spinach to the vegetables and mix, mashing down with a fork.

3 Using a sharp knife, finely chop the green chilies and fresh cilantro leaves.

4 Mix the finely chopped chilies and cilantro with the ginger, garlic, ground coriander, turmeric, and salt.

5 Blend the spice mixture into the vegetables, mixing with a fork to make a paste.

6 Scatter the bread crumbs onto a large plate.

7 Break off 10–12 small balls from the spice paste. Flatten them between the palms of your hands to make flat patties.

8 Dip each patty in the bread crumbs, coating well.

9 Heat the oil in a heavy skillet and shallow-fry the patties, in batches, until golden brown, turning occasionally. Transfer to serving plates and garnish with fresh chili strips. Serve hot.

Curried Okra

This is a delicious dry bhujia *(vegetarian curry) that should be served hot with chapatis (see page 180). As okra is so tasty, it does not need many spices.*

Serves 4

INGREDIENTS

1 pound okra	3 fresh green chilies, finely chopped	1 tomato, sliced
2/3 cup oil	2 curry leaves	2 tbsp lemon juice
2 medium onions, sliced	1 tsp salt	fresh cilantro leaves

1 Rinse the okra and drain thoroughly. Using a sharp knife, chop and discard the ends of the okra. Cut the okra into 1-inch-long pieces.

2 Heat the oil in a large, heavy skillet. Add the onions, fresh green chilies, curry leaves, and salt and mix together. Stir-fry the vegetables for 5 minutes.

3 Gradually add the okra, mixing in gently with a slotted spoon. Stir-fry the vegetable mixture over a medium heat for 12–15 minutes.

4 Add the sliced tomato to the skillet and sprinkle sparingly with the lemon juice.

5 Garnish with cilantro leaves, cover, and simmer for 3–5 minutes.

6 Transfer to serving plates and serve hot.

COOK'S TIP

Okra has a remarkable glutinous quality which naturally thickens curries and casseroles.

COOK'S TIP

When you buy fresh okra, make sure they are not shriveled and that they do not have any brown spots. Fresh okra will keep, tightly wrapped, for up to 3 days in the refrigerator.

Spinach & Cheese Curry

*This vegetarian curry is full of protein and iron. Serve as a side dish with
meat curries or as part of a vegetarian menu. Panir is a type of cheese.*

Serves 4

INGREDIENTS

1¹/₄ cups oil
7 ounces panir, cubed (see
   Cook's Tip)

3 tomatoes, sliced
1 tsp ground cumin
1¹/₂ tsp ground chili powder

1 tsp salt
14 ounces fresh spinach
3 fresh green chilies

1 Heat the oil in a large skillet.
Add the cubed panir and
fry, stirring occasionally, until
golden brown.

2 Remove the panir from the
skillet with a slotted spoon
and set aside to drain on paper
towels.

3 Add the tomatoes to the
remaining oil in the skillet
and stir-fry, breaking up the
tomatoes, for 5 minutes.

4 Add the ground cumin, chili
powder, and salt to the pan
and mix together well.

5 Add the spinach to the skillet
and stir-fry over a low heat
for 7–10 minutes.

6 Add the fresh green chilies
and the panir and cook,
stirring, for a further 2 minutes.

7 Transfer to serving plates and
serve hot with pooris or plain
boiled rice.

VARIATION

*You could used frozen spinach in
this recipe. It should be thawed and
squeezed dry before using.*

COOK'S TIP

*To make panir, boil 4¹/₂ cups milk
slowly over a low heat, then add
2 tbsp lemon juice, stirring
continuously and gently until the
milk thickens and begins to curdle.
Strain the curdled milk through a
fine strainer. Set aside under
a heavy weight for about
1¹/₂–2 hours to press to a flat
shape about ¹/₂ inch thick. Once
set, the panir can be cut,
like cheese, into whatever
shape is required.*

Vegetable Curry

*This colorful and interesting mixture of vegetables, cooked in a spicy sauce, is excellent
served with pulao rice (see page 158) and nan bread (see page 178).*

Serves 4

INGREDIENTS

8 ounces turnips or rutabaga, peeled
1 eggplant, leaf end trimmed
12 ounces new potatoes, scrubbed
8 ounces cauliflower
8 ounces button mushrooms
1 large onion
8 ounces carrots, peeled
6 tbsp vegetable ghee or oil
2 garlic cloves, crushed

2-inch piece fresh ginger root,
  chopped finely
1–2 fresh green chilies, seeded and
  chopped
1 tbsp paprika
2 tsp ground coriander
1 tbsp mild or medium curry powder
  or paste
1³/₄ cups vegetable stock
14 ounce can chopped tomatoes

1 green bell pepper, seeded and sliced
1 tbsp cornstarch
²/₃ cup coconut milk
2–3 tbsp ground almonds
salt
fresh cilantro sprigs, to garnish

1 Cut the turnips or rutabaga,
eggplant and potatoes into
¹/₂-inch cubes. Divide the
cauliflower into small florets.
Leave the mushrooms whole, or
slice thickly if desired. Slice the
onion and carrots.

2 Heat the ghee or oil in a large
saucepan, add the onion,
turnip or rutabaga, potato,
cauliflower, and carrots and cook
gently for 3 minutes, stirring
frequently. Add the garlic, ginger,
chilies, paprika, ground coriander,
and curry powder or paste and
cook for 1 minute, stirring.

3 Add the stock, tomatoes,
eggplant, and mushrooms and
season with salt. Cover and
simmer gently for about
30 minutes, or until tender,
stirring occasionally. Add the green
bell pepper, cover, and continue
cooking for a further 5 minutes.

4 Smoothly blend the
cornstarch with the coconut
milk and stir into the mixture. Add
the ground almonds and simmer
for 2 minutes, stirring all the time.
Season with salt, if necessary.
Transfer to warm serving plates
and serve hot, garnished with
sprigs of fresh cilantro.

Stuffed Rice Crêpes

Dosas (crêpes) are widely eaten in southern India. They can be served either on their own with a chutney or, as here, with a vegetable filling, when they are known as masala dosa.

Makes 6–8

INGREDIENTS

1 cup rice and $^1/_4$ cup *urid dhal*, or
 1$^1/_4$ cups ground rice and $^1/_2$ cup
 urid dhal flour (*ata*)
2–1$^1/_2$ cups water
1 tsp salt
4 tbsp oil

FILLING:
4 medium potatoes, diced
3 fresh green chilies, chopped
$^1/_2$ tsp turmeric
1 tsp salt
$^2/_3$ cup oil
1 tsp mustard and onion seeds

3 dried red chilies
4 curry leaves
2 tbsp lemon juice

1 To make the *dosas* (crêpes), soak the rice and *urid dhal* for 3 hours. Grind the rice and *urid dhal* to a smooth consistency, adding water if necessary. Set aside for a further 3 hours to ferment. Alternatively, if you are using ground rice and *urid dhal* flour (*ata*), mix together in a bowl. Add the water and salt and stir until a batter is formed.

2 Heat about 1 tbsp of oil in a large, nonstick, skillet. Using a ladle, spoon the batter into the skillet. Tilt the skillet to spread the mixture over the base. Cover and cook over a medium heat for about 2 minutes. Remove the lid and turn the *dosa* over very carefully. Pour a little oil around the edge, cover, and cook for a further 2 minutes. Repeat with the remaining batter.

3 To make the filling, boil the potatoes in a pan of water. Add the chilies, turmeric, and salt and cook until the potatoes are soft enough to be lightly mashed.

4 Heat the oil in a saucepan and fry the mustard and onion seeds, dried red chilies, and curry leaves for about 1 minute. Pour the spice mixture over the mashed potatoes, then sprinkle with the lemon juice, and mix well. Spoon the potato filling on one half of the *dosas* (crêpes) and fold the other half over the filling. Serve hot.

Potatoes with Spices & Onions

Masala aloo are potatoes cooked in spices and onions. Semi-dry when cooked, they make an excellent accompaniment to almost any meat or vegetable curry.

Serves 4

INGREDIENTS

6 tbsp oil
2 medium-size onions,
   finely chopped
1 tsp finely chopped fresh
   ginger root
1 tsp crushed garlic
1 tsp chili powder
$1^1/_2$ tsp ground cumin

$1^1/_2$ tsp ground coriander
1 tsp salt
14 ounce can new potatoes
1 tbsp lemon juice

BAGHAAR:
3 tbsp oil
3 dried red chilies

$^1/_2$ tsp onion seeds
$^1/_2$ tsp mustard seeds
$^1/_2$ tsp fenugreek seeds

TO GARNISH:
fresh cilantro leaves
1 fresh green chili, finely chopped

1 Heat the oil in a large saucepan. Add the onions and sauté until golden brown. Reduce the heat, add the ginger, garlic, chili powder, ground cumin, ground coriander, and salt and stir-fry for about 1 minute. Remove the pan from the heat and set aside until required.

2 Drain the water from the potatoes. Add the potatoes to the onion and spice mixture.

Sprinkle the lemon juice into the pan and mix well.

3 To make the *baghaar*, heat the oil in a separate pan. Add the red chilies, onion seeds, mustard seeds, and fenugreek seeds and fry until the seeds turn a shade darker. Remove the pan from the heat and pour the *baghaar* over the potatoes.

4 Garnish with cilantro leaves and fresh chilies.

COOK'S TIP

You could also serve these spicy potatoes and onions, for a change, with roast lamb or lamb chops.

White Radish Curry

This is a rather unusual recipe for a vegetarian curry. The dish is good served hot with chapatis (see page 180).

Serves 4

INGREDIENTS

1 pound white radish, preferably
  with leaves
1 tbsp *moong dhal*

2¹/₂ cups water
1 medium onion
²/₃ cup oil

1 tsp crushed garlic
1 tsp dried red chilies, crushed
1 tsp salt

1 Rinse, peel, and roughly slice the white radish together with its leaves (if using).

2 Place the white radish, the leaves (if using), and the *moong dhal* in a pan and pour in the water. Bring to a boil until the white radish is soft enough to be handled.

3 Drain the white radish thoroughly and squeeze out any excess water, using your hands.

4 Using a sharp knife, slice the onion thinly.

5 Heat the oil in a saucepan. Add the onion, garlic, crushed red chilies, and salt and fry, stirring occasionally, until the onions have softened and turned a light golden brown color.

6 Stir the white radish mixture into the spiced onion mixture and mix to combine well. Reduce the heat and continue cooking, stirring frequently, for about 3–5 minutes.

7 Transfer the white radish curry to warm individual serving plates and serve hot with chapatis (see page 180).

COOK'S TIP

The vegetable used in this recipe, white radish, looks a bit like a parsnip without the tapering end and is now sold in most supermarkets as well as in Indian and Pakistani grocery stores.

Eggplants in Pickling Spices

This is a very versatile dish that will go with almost anything and can be served warm or cold. Perfect as an "extra" for a dinner party, this is another dish that originates from Hyderabad in southern India.

Serves 4

INGREDIENTS

2 tsp ground coriander

2 tsp ground cumin

2 tsp shredded coconut

2 tsp sesame seeds

1 tsp mixed mustard and onion seeds

1¼ cups oil

3 medium onions, sliced

1 tsp finely chopped fresh
  ginger root

1 tsp crushed garlic

½ tsp turmeric

1½ tsp chili powder

1½ tsp salt

3 medium eggplants, halved
  lengthwise

1 tbsp tamarind paste

1¼ cups water

BAGHAAR:

1 tsp mixed onion and mustard seeds

1 tsp cumin seeds

4 dried red chilies

⅔ cup oil

cilantro leaves

1 fresh green chili, finely chopped

3 hard-boiled eggs, halved, to garnish

1 Dry-fry the coriander, cumin, coconut, sesame seeds, and mustard and onion seeds in a pan. Grind in a mortar with a pestle or in a food processor and set aside.

2 Heat the oil in a skillet and fry the onions until golden. Reduce the heat and add the ginger, garlic, turmeric, chili powder, and salt, stirring. Cool, then grind this mixture to form a smooth paste.

3 Make 4 cuts across each eggplant half. Blend the spices with the onion paste. Spoon this mixture into the slits in the eggplants.

4 In a bowl, mix the tamarind paste and 3 tbsp water to make a fine paste and set aside.

5 For the *baghaar*, fry the onion and mustard seeds, cumin seeds, and chilies in the oil.

6 Reduce the heat, gently place the stuffed eggplants into the heated *baghaar*, and stir gently. Stir in the tamarind paste and the rest of the water and cook over a medium heat for 15–20 minutes. Add the cilantro and fresh green chilies.

7 When cool, transfer to a serving dish and serve garnished with the hard-boiled eggs.

Dumplings in Yogurt Sauce

Gram flour flavors and thickens the sauce in this recipe, and a baghaar (seasoned oil dressing) is added just before serving. It makes a mouth-watering accompaniment to any meal.

Serves 4

INGREDIENTS

DUMPLINGS:
$3/4$ cup gram flour
1 tsp chili powder
$1/2$ tsp salt
$1/2$ tsp baking soda
1 medium onion, finely chopped
2 fresh green chilies
fresh cilantro leaves
$2/3$ cup water
$1 1/4$ cups oil

YOGURT SAUCE:
$1 1/4$ cups unsweetened yogurt
3 tbsp gram flour
$2/3$ cup water
1 tsp chopped fresh ginger root
1 tsp crushed garlic
$1 1/2$ tsp chili powder
$1 1/2$ tsp salt
$1/2$ tsp turmeric
1 tsp ground coriander
1 tsp ground cumin

SEASONED DRESSING:
$2/3$ cup oil
1 tsp white cumin seeds
6 dried red chilies

1 To make the dumplings, sift the gram flour into a large bowl. Add the chili powder, salt, baking soda, onion, fresh green chilies, and cilantro and mix. Add the water and mix to form a thick paste. Heat the oil in a skillet. Place teaspoonfuls of the paste in the oil and fry over a medium heat, turning once, until crisp and golden brown. Set aside.

2 To make the sauce, place the yogurt in a bowl and beat in the gram flour and water. Add all the spices and mix well.

3 Push this mixture through a large strainer into a saucepan. Bring to a boil over a low heat, stirring continuously. If the yogurt sauce becomes too thick, add a little extra water.

4 Pour the sauce into a deep serving dish and arrange all the dumplings on top. Set aside and keep warm.

5 To make the dressing, heat the oil in a skillet. Add the white cumin seeds and the dried red chilies and fry until darker in color. Pour the dressing over the dumplings and serve hot.

Potato Curry

Served hot with pooris (see page 184), this curry makes an excellent brunch with mango chutney (see page 218) as an accompaniment.

Serves 4

INGREDIENTS

3 medium potatoes
$^2/_3$ cup oil
1 tsp onion seeds
$^1/_2$ tsp fennel seeds

4 curry leaves
1 tsp ground cumin
1 tsp ground coriander
1 tsp chili powder

1 pinch turmeric
1 tsp salt
$1^1/_2$ tsp *aamchoor* (dried
  mango powder)

1 Peel and rinse the potatoes. Using a sharp knife, cut each potato into six slices.

2 Boil the potato slices in a saucepan of water until just cooked, but not mushy (test by piercing with a sharp knife). Drain and set aside until required.

3 In a separate saucepan heat the oil. Reduce the heat and add the onion seeds, fennel seeds, and curry leaves, stirring.

4 Remove the pan from the heat and add the ground cumin, coriander, chili powder, turmeric, salt, and aamchoor (dried mango powder), stirring well to combine.

5 Return the pan to the heat and stir-fry the mixture for about 1 minute.

6 Pour this mixture over the cooked potatoes, mix together, and stir-fry over a low heat for about 5 minutes.

7 Transfer the potato curry to warm serving dishes and serve immediately.

COOK'S TIP

Traditionally, cream of wheat dessert (see page 244) is served to follow potato curry.

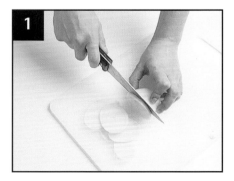

Zucchini & Fenugreek Seeds

This delicious curry contains fenugreek seeds which have a beautiful aroma and a distinctive taste.

Serves 4

INGREDIENTS

6 tbsp oil
1 medium onion, finely chopped
3 fresh green chilies, finely chopped
1 tsp finely chopped fresh
   ginger root

1 tsp crushed garlic
1 tsp chili powder
3$\frac{1}{2}$ cups sliced zucchini
2 tomatoes, sliced

fresh cilantro leaves
2 tsp fenugreek seeds
fresh cilantro, to garnish

1 Heat the oil in a large skillet.

2 Add the onion, fresh green chilies, ginger, garlic, and chili powder to the skillet, stirring well to combine.

3 Add the sliced zucchini and the sliced tomatoes to the skillet and stir-fry for 5–7 minutes.

4 Add the cilantro and fenugreek seeds to the zucchini mixture in the pan and stir-fry for a further 5 minutes.

5 Remove the skillet from the heat and transfer the zucchini and fenugreek seed mixture to warm serving dishes. Garnish with fresh cilantro and serve hot with chapatis.

COOK'S TIP

Both the leaves and seeds of fenugreek are used, but the stalks and root should be discarded, as they have a bitter taste. Fresh fenugreek is sold in bunches. Fenugreek seeds are flat and yellowish brown in color.

VARIATION

You could use coriander seeds instead of the fenugreek seeds, if desired.

Green Pumpkin Curry

The Indian pumpkin used in this curry is long and green and sold by weight.
It can easily be bought from any Indian or Pakistani grocery stores.

Serves 4

INGREDIENTS

$^2/_3$ cup oil
2 medium-size onions, sliced
$^1/_2$ tsp white cumin seeds
$3^1/_2$ cups diced green pumpkin

1 tsp *aamchoor* (dried
  mango powder)
1 tsp finely chopped fresh
  ginger root

1 tsp crushed garlic
1 tsp crushed red chili
$^1/_2$ tsp salt
$1^1/_4$ cups water

1 Heat the oil in a large heavy-based skillet. Add the onions and cumin seeds and fry, stirring occasionally, until a light golden brown color.

2 Add the diced pumpkin to the pan and stir-fry for 3–5 minutes over a low heat.

3 Mix the aamchoor (dried mango powder), ginger, garlic, chili, and salt together.

4 Add the spice mixture to the onion mixture, stirring well to combine.

5 Add the water, cover, and cook over a low heat for 10–15 minutes, stirring occasionally.

6 Transfer to serving plates and serve with gram flour bread (see page 176).

COOK'S TIP

Cumin seeds are popular with Indian cooks because of their warm, pungent flavor and aroma. The seeds are sold whole or ground, and are usually included as one of the flavorings in garam masala.

VARIATION

You can use ordinary pumpkin for this recipe, if desired.

Potatoes & Peas

This quick and easy-to-prepare vegetarian dish can be served either as an accompaniment or on its own with chapatis (see page 180).

Serves 2–4

INGREDIENTS

²/₃ cup oil
3 medium onions, sliced
1 tsp crushed garlic
1 tsp finely chopped fresh
   ginger root

1 tsp chili powder
¹/₂ tsp turmeric
1 tsp salt
2 fresh fresh green chilies,
   finely chopped

1¹/₄ cups water
3 medium potatoes
1 cup peas
fresh cilantro leaves,
   to garnish

1 Heat the oil in a large skillet.

2 Add the onions to the skillet and fry, stirring occasionally, until the onions are golden brown in color.

3 Mix together the garlic, ginger, chili powder, turmeric, salt, and fresh green chilies. Add the spice mixture to the onions in the skillet.

4 Stir in ²/₃ cup of the water, cover, and cook until the onions are cooked through.

5 Meanwhile, cut the potatoes into six slices each, using a sharp knife.

6 Add the potato slices to the mixture in the skillet and stir-fry for 5 minutes.

7 Add the peas and the remaining ²/₃ cup of the water to the skillet, cover, and cook for 7–10 minutes.

8 Transfer the potatoes and peas to warm serving plates and serve garnished with fresh cilantro leaves.

COOK'S TIP

Turmeric is an aromatic root that is dried and ground to produce the distinctive bright yellow powder used in many Indian dishes. It has a warm, aromatic smell and a full, somewhat musty taste.

Garbanzo Bean Curry

This curry is very popular among the many vegetarian people in India. There are many different ways of cooking garbanzo beans, but this version is probably one of the most delicious.

Serves 4

INGREDIENTS

6 tbsp oil
2 medium onions, sliced
1 tsp finely chopped fresh
    ginger root
1 tsp ground cumin

1 tsp ground coriander
1 tsp crushed garlic
1 tsp chili powder
2 fresh fresh green chilies
fresh cilantro leaves

²/₃ cup water
1 large potato
14 ounce can garbanzo
    beans, drained
1 tbsp lemon juice

1 Heat the oil in a large saucepan.

2 Add the onions to the pan and sauté until golden brown.

3 Reduce the heat, add the ginger, ground cumin, ground coriander, garlic, chili powder, fresh green chilies, and fresh cilantro leaves to the pan and stir-fry for 2 minutes.

4 Add the water to the mixture in the pan and stir well to mix.

5 Using a sharp knife, cut the potato into small cubes.

6 Add the potatoes and the drained garbanzo beans to the mixture in the pan, cover, and simmer, stirring occasionally, for 5–7 minutes.

7 Sprinkle the lemon juice over the curry.

8 Transfer the garbanzo bean curry to serving dishes. Serve the curry hot with chapati, if desired.

COOK'S TIP

Using canned garbanzo beans saves time, but you can use dried garbanzo beans if desired. Soak them overnight, then boil them for 15–20 minutes, or until soft.

Egg Curry

This curry can be made very quickly. It can either be served
as a side dish or with paratas (see page 174) as a light lunch.

Serves 4

INGREDIENTS

4 tbsp oil
1 medium onion, sliced
1 fresh red chili, finely chopped
$^{1}/_{2}$ tsp chili powder

$^{1}/_{2}$ tsp finely chopped fresh
  ginger root
$^{1}/_{2}$ tsp crushed garlic
4 medium eggs

1 firm tomato, sliced
fresh cilantro leaves

1 Heat the oil in a large saucepan.

2 Add the onion to the pan and sauté until just softened and a light golden color.

3 Add the red chili, chili powder, ginger, and garlic and stir-fry the mixture, over a low heat, for about 1 minute.

4 Add the eggs and tomatoes to the mixture in the pan and continue cooking, stirring to break up the eggs when they begin to cook, for 3–5 minutes.

5 Sprinkle the fresh cilantro leaves into the pan.

6 Transfer the egg curry to serving plates and serve hot with paratas (see page 174), if desired.

COOK'S TIP

Both the leaves and and finely chopped stems of cilantro are used in Indian cooking, to flavor dishes and as edible garnishes. It has a very distinctive and pronounced taste.

COOK'S TIP

Eggs contain high-quality protein, fat, iron, and vitamins A, B, and D, although they are also high in cholesterol.

Mixed Vegetables

*You can make this recipe with any vegetables you choose,
but the combination below is ideal.*

Serves 4

INGREDIENTS

1¼ cups oil
1 tsp mustard seeds
1 tsp onion seeds
½ tsp white cumin seeds
3–4 curry leaves, chopped
1 pound onions,
   finely chopped
3 medium tomatoes, chopped

½ red, ½ green bell pepper, sliced
1 tsp finely chopped fresh
   ginger root
1 tsp crushed garlic
1 tsp chili powder
¼ tsp turmeric
1 tsp salt
2 cups water

2 medium potatoes, peeled and cut
   into pieces
½ cauliflower, cut into
   small florets
4 medium carrots, peeled and sliced
3 fresh green chilies, finely chopped
fresh cilantro leaves
1 tbsp lemon juice

1 Heat the oil in a large saucepan. Add the mustard, onion, and white cumin seeds, together with the curry leaves, and fry until they turn a shade darker.

2 Add the onions to the pan and fry over a medium heat until golden brown.

3 Add the tomatoes and bell pepper halves and stir-fry for about 5 minutes.

4 Add the ginger, garlic, chili powder, turmeric, and salt and mix well.

5 Add 1¼ cups of the water, cover, and simmer for about 10–12 minutes, stirring occasionally.

6 Add the potatoes, cauliflower, carrots, fresh green chilies, and cilantro leaves and stir-fry for about 5 minutes.

7 Add the remaining ⅔ cup of water and the lemon juice, stirring to combine. Cover and simmer for about 15 minutes, stirring occasionally.

8 Transfer the mixed vegetables to serving plates and serve immediately.

Potato & Cauliflower Curry

Potatoes and cauliflower go very well together. Served with a dhal
and pooris (see page 184), this dish makes a perfect vegetarian meal.

Serves 4

INGREDIENTS

²/₃ cup oil
¹/₂ tsp white cumin seeds
4 dried red chilies
2 medium onions, sliced
1 tsp finely chopped fresh
   ginger root

1 tsp crushed garlic
1 tsp chili powder
1 tsp salt
1 pinch of turmeric
3 medium potatoes

¹/₂ cauliflower, cut into
   small florets
2 fresh green chilies (optional)
fresh cilantro leaves
²/₃ cup water

1   Heat the oil in a large saucepan.

2   Add the white cumin seeds and dried red chilies to the pan, stirring to mix.

3   Add the onions to the pan and fry, stirring occasionally, until golden brown.

4   Mix the ginger, garlic, chili powder, salt, and turmeric together. Add the spice mixture to the onions and stir-fry for about 2 minutes.

5   Add the potatoes and cauliflower to the onion and spice mixture, stirring to coat the vegetables in the spice mixture.

6   Reduce the heat and add the fresh green chilies (if using), fresh cilantro leaves, and water to the pan. Cover and simmer the mixture for about 10–15 minutes.

7   Transfer the potato and cauliflower curry to warm serving plates and serve immediately.

COOK'S TIP

Always handle chilies with caution, preferably wearing protective gloves because the juices are extremely pungent. Wash your hands thoroughly after preparing and handling chilies and do not allow your fingers near your eyes, as this can be very painful.

Dry Split Okra

This is an unusual way of cooking this delicious vegetable. The dish is dry when cooked, and should be served hot with chapatis (see page 180) and a dhal.

Serves 4

INGREDIENTS

1 pound okra
²/₃ cup oil
¹/₂ cup dried onions

2 tsp *aamchoor* (dried
    mango powder)
1 tsp ground cumin

1 tsp chili powder
1 tsp salt

1 Prepare the okra by cutting the ends off and discarding them. Carefully split them down the middle without cutting through completely.

2 Heat the oil in a large saucepan. Add the dried onions and fry until crisp.

3 Remove the onions from the pan with a slotted spoon and set aside to drain thoroughly on paper towels.

4 When cool enough to handle, roughly tear the dried onions and place in a large bowl.

5 Add the *aamchoor* (dried mango), ground cumin, chili powder, and salt to the dried onions and blend well together.

6 Spoon the onion mixture into the split okra.

7 Reheat the oil in the saucepan.

8 Gently add the okra to the hot oil and cook over a low heat for about 10–12 minutes.

9 Transfer the cooked okra to a serving dish and serve immediately.

COOK'S TIP

Ground cumin has a warm, pungent aromatic flavor and is used extensively in Indian cooking. It is a good standby.

Tomato Curry

This vegetarian tomato curry is served topped with a few hard-boiled eggs. It makes a lovely accompaniment to almost any meal, and goes well with spiced rice and lentils (see page 154).

Serves 4

INGREDIENTS

14 ounce can tomatoes
1 tsp finely chopped fresh
  ginger root
1 tsp crushed garlic
1 tsp chili powder
1 tsp salt
$^1/_2$ tsp ground coriander

$^1/_2$ tsp ground cumin
4 tbsp oil
$^1/_2$ tsp onion seeds
$^1/_2$ tsp mustard seeds
$^1/_2$ tsp fenugreek seeds
1 pinch white cumin seeds
3 dried red chilies

2 tbsp lemon juice
3 eggs, hard-boiled
fresh cilantro leaves

1 Place the tomatoes in a large mixing bowl.

2 Add the ginger, garlic, chili powder, salt, ground coriander, and ground cumin to the tomatoes and blend well.

3 Heat the oil in a saucepan. Add the onion, mustard, fenugreek, and white cumin seeds, and the dried red chilies, and stir-fry for about 1 minute. Remove the pan from the heat.

4 Add the tomato mixture to the spicy oil mixture and return to the heat. Stir-fry the mixture for about 3 minutes, then reduce the heat and cook with the lid ajar for 7–10 minutes, stirring occasionally.

5 Sprinkle the lemon juice sparingly over the mixture.

6 Transfer the tomato curry to a serving dish, set aside, and keep warm until required.

7 Shell and halve the hard-boiled eggs, then gently add them, yolk side down, to the tomato curry.

8 Garnish with fresh cilantro leaves and serve hot.

COOK'S TIP

This tomato curry can be made in advance and frozen, as it freezes particularly well.

Breads & Grains

The most common Indian breads are chapati, paratas, and poori, all of which can be made with whole-wheat flour—so they are very healthy foods. These three breads are cooked almost every day in most Indian households. Indian breads are made as individual portions, and you may want to allow two per person.

Rice is served with almost every meal in India, so the Indians have created a variety of ways of cooking it. The aim is to produce dry, separate grained rice that is cooked yet still has some "bite" to it. Basmati rice cooks very well and gives an excellent result. It is best to soak it for 20–30 minutes before cooking, to prevent the grains from sticking to each other. As a rough guide, allow about $2/3$ cup rice per person.

There are at least thirty different types of lentil in India, but the four most commonly used are moong, masoor, chana, and urid. Rich in protein, lentils make ideal accompaniments to vegetable curries, which otherwise lack protein. Lentils are also delicious cooked with a variety of meats. Before cooking, wash the lentils at least twice and if you have time, soak them for 3 hours–this will also cut down on the cooking time.

Lemon Dhal

This dhal *is eaten almost every day in most households in Hyderabad in India. Traditionally, it is cooked with tamarind, but lemon juice is easier and more colorful.*

Serves 4

INGREDIENTS

$^1/_2$ cup *masoor dhal*
1 tsp finely chopped fresh
   ginger root
1 tsp crushed garlic
1 tsp chili powder
$^1/_2$ tsp turmeric

2 cups water
1 tsp salt
3 tbsp lemon juice
2 fresh green chilies
fresh cilantro leaves

BAGHAAR:
$^2/_3$ cup oil
4 whole garlic cloves
6 dried red chilies
1 tsp white cumin seeds

1 Rinse the *masoor dhal* and place in a large saucepan.

2 Add the ginger, garlic, chili powder, and turmeric to the dhal. Stir in 1$^1/_4$ cups of the water and bring to a boil over a medium heat with the lid left slightly ajar. Cook until the *dhal* is soft enough to be mashed.

3 Mash the *dhal*. Add the salt, lemon juice, and $^2/_3$ cup of the water, stir, and mix well. It should be of a fairly smooth consistency.

4 Add the fresh green chilies and fresh cilantro leaves to the *dhal* and set aside.

5 To make the *baghaar*, heat the oil in a pan. Add the garlic, red chilies, and white cumin seeds and fry for about 1 minute. Turn off the heat, then when it is slightly cooler, pour the *baghaar* over the *dhal*. If the *dhal* is too runny, cook over a medium heat with the lid off for 3–5 minutes.

6 Transfer to a serving dish and serve hot.

COOK'S TIP

This dish is a good accompaniment to beef khorma with almonds (see page 50).

White Lentils

This dhal *is dry when cooked, so try serving it with a* baghaar *(seasoned oil dressing).*
It makes an excellent accompaniment to any meal of khorma *and chapatis (see page 180).*

Serves 2–4

INGREDIENTS

$^1/_2$ cup *urid dhal*
1 tsp finely chopped fresh
    ginger root
2$^1/_2$ cups water

1 tsp salt
1 tsp pepper
2 tbsp pure or vegetable ghee
2 cloves garlic, peeled

2 fresh red chilies, finely chopped
fresh mint leaves, to garnish

1 Rinse the lentils twice, removing any stones.

2 Place the lentils and ginger in a large saucepan.

3 Add the water and bring to a boil, covered, over a medium heat for about 30 minutes. Check to see whether the lentils are cooked by rubbing them between your finger and thumb. If they are still a little hard in the middle, cook for a further 5–7 minutes. If necessary, remove the lid and cook until any remaining water has evaporated.

4 Add the salt and coarsely ground black pepper to the lentils, mix well, and set aside.

5 Heat the ghee in a separate saucepan. Add the cloves of garlic and chopped red chilies, and stir well to mix.

6 Pour the garlic and chili mixture over the lentils and then garnish with the fresh mint leaves.

7 Transfer the white lentils to serving dishes and serve hot with chapatis (see page 180).

COOK'S TIP

Urid dhal *are small, round white split lentils, which are popular with northern Indians. Dhals are usually labeled simply "lentils" in most supermarkets.*

Onion Dhal

This dhal is semi-dry when cooked, so it is best to serve it with a curry that has a sauce.
Ordinary onions can be used as a substitute if scallions are not available.

Serves 4

INGREDIENTS

$^1/_2$ cup *masoor dhal*
6 tbsp oil
1 small bunch scallions, trimmed and
   chopped, including the green part

1 tsp finely chopped fresh
   ginger root
1 tsp crushed garlic
$^1/_2$ tsp chili powder
$^1/_2$ tsp turmeric

$1^1/_4$ cups water
1 tsp salt
1 fresh green chili,
   finely chopped
fresh cilantro leaves

1 Rinse the lentils and set aside until required.

2 Heat the oil in a saucepan. Add the scallions to the pan and sauté, stirring occasionally, until lightly browned.

3 Reduce the heat and add the ginger, garlic, chili powder, and turmeric to the pan. Stir-fry the scallions with the spices, stirring to combine.

4 Add the lentils and mix to blend together.

5 Add the water to the lentil mixture in the pan, reduce the heat further, and cook for 20–25 minutes.

6 When the lentils are cooked thoroughly, add the salt and stir gently with a wooden spoon to combine.

7 Garnish the onion lentils with the chopped fresh green chilies and fresh cilantro leaves. Transfer the onion lentils to a warm serving dish and serve immediately.

COOK'S TIP

Masoor dhal *are small, round, pale orange split lentils. They turn a pale yellow color when cooked.*

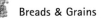

Oil-Dressed Dhal

This dhal *is given a* tarka, *or* baghaar *(seasoned-oil dressing), just before serving, of ghee, onion, and a combination of seeds. It has a thick sauce when cooked.*

Serves 4

INGREDIENTS

5 tbsp *masoor dhal*
4 tbsp *moong dhal*
2 cups water
1 tsp finely chopped fresh
   ginger root
1 tsp crushed garlic

2 fresh red chilies, chopped
1 tsp salt

TARKA (BAGHAAR):
2 tbsp ghee
1 medium onion, sliced

mixed mustard and onion seeds

---

1 Rinse the lentils, removing any stones.

2 Place the lentils in a large saucepan and add the water, stirring. Add the ginger, garlic, and fresh red chilies and bring to a boil over a medium heat, half covered with a lid, until they are soft enough to be mashed (about 15–20 minutes).

3 Mash the lentils and add more water if necessary to form a thick sauce.

4 Add the salt to the lentil mixture and stir to combine. Transfer the lentils to a heatproof serving dish.

5 Just before serving, melt the ghee in a small saucepan. Add the onion and sauté until golden brown. Add the mixed mustard and onion seeds and stir to mix thoroughly.

6 Pour the onion mixture over the lentils while still hot. Serve immediately.

COOK'S TIP

This dish makes a very good accompaniment, especially for a dry vegetarian or meat curry. It also freezes well—simply reheat it in a saucepan or covered in the oven.

Black-Eye Peas

This is semi-dry when cooked, and is very good served with a few drops of lemon juice or with chapatis (see page 180) and a wet curry.

Serves 4

INGREDIENTS

1 cup black-eye peas
1¹/₄ cups oil
2 medium onions, sliced
1 tsp finely chopped fresh
   ginger root
1 tsp crushed garlic

1 tsp chili powder
1¹/₂ tsp salt
1¹/₂ tsp ground coriander
1¹/₂ tsp ground cumin
²/₃ cup water
2 fresh green chilies

fresh cilantro leaves
1 tbsp lemon juice

1 Rinse and soak the black-eye peas in a bowl of cold water overnight.

2 Drain and place the black-eye peas in a pan of water and bring to a boil over a low heat for about 30 minutes. Drain the peas thoroughly and set aside.

3 Heat the oil in a pan. Add the onions and fry until golden brown. Add the ginger, garlic, chili powder, salt, ground coriander, and ground cumin and stir-fry the mixture for 3–5 minutes.

4 Add the water to the pan, cover, and cook the mixture until all of the water has completely evaporated.

5 Add the boiled black-eye peas, fresh green chilies, and cilantro leaves to the onions and stir to blend together. Stir-fry the black-eye pea mixture for 3–5 minutes.

6 Transfer the black-eye peas to a serving dish and sprinkle the lemon juice over them. Serve hot or cold.

COOK'S TIP

Black-eye peas are oval-shaped, gray or beige peas with a dark dot in the center. They have a slightly smoky flavor. They are sold canned as well as dried.

Dry Moong Dhal

*A baghaar (seasoned-oil dressing) of butter, dried red chilies, and white cumin seeds
goes well with this dhal. It is simple to cook and tastes very good.*

Serves 4

INGREDIENTS

1 cup *moong dhal*
1 tsp finely chopped fresh
 ginger root
$1/2$ tsp ground cumin
$1/2$ tsp ground coriander

1 tsp crushed garlic
$1/2$ tsp chili powder
$2^1/2$ cups water
1 tsp salt

BAGHAAR:
7 tbsp sweet butter
5 dried red chilies
1 tsp white cumin seeds

1 Rinse the lentils, removing
any stones.

2 Place the lentils in a pan. Add
the ginger, ground cumin,
ground coriander, garlic, and chili
powder, and stir to mix.

3 Pour in the water to cover the
lentil mixture. Cook over a
medium heat, stirring, until the
lentils are soft, but not mushy.

4 Add the salt to the lentils and
stir to mix. Transfer to a
serving dish and keep warm.

5 Meanwhile, make the *baghaar*.
Melt the butter in a saucepan.
Add the dried red chilies and white
cumin seeds and fry until they
begin to pop.

6 Pour the *baghaar* over the
lentils and serve hot with
chapati and a vegetable or
meat curry.

COOK'S TIP

*Dried red chilies are the quickest
way to add heat to a dish.*

COOK'S TIP

*Moong dhal are teardrop-
shaped yellow split lentils, more
popular in northern India
than in the south.*

Spinach & Chana Dhal

*An attractive dish, this makes a good vegetarian accompaniment to almost any meal.
For a good contrast in color and taste, cook a tomato curry (see page 134) with this.*

Serves 4–6

INGREDIENTS

4 tbsp *chana dhal*

6 tbsp oil

1 tsp mixed onion and mustard seeds

4 dried red chilies

14–16 ounce can spinach, drained

1 tsp finely chopped fresh
  ginger root

1 tsp ground coriander

1 tsp ground cumin

1 tsp salt

1 tsp chili powder

2 tbsp lemon juice

1 fresh green chili, to garnish

1 Soak the *chana dhal* in a bowl of warm water for at least 3 hours, preferably overnight.

2 Place the lentils in a saucepan, cover with water, and boil for 30 minutes.

3 Heat the oil in a saucepan. Add the mixed onion and mustard seeds and dried red chilies and fry, stirring constantly, until they turn a shade darker.

4 Add the drained spinach to the pan, mixing gently.

5 Add the ginger, ground coriander, ground cumin, salt and chili powder to the pan. Reduce the heat and gently stir-fry the mixture for 7–10 minutes.

6 Add the lentils to the pan and blend into the spinach mixture well, stirring gently so that it does not break up.

7 Transfer the mixture to a serving dish. Sprinkle the lemon juice over the top and garnish with the fresh green chili. Serve immediately.

COOK'S TIP

Very similar in appearance to moong dhal—*the yellow split peas—*chana dhal *has slightly less shiny grains. It is used as a binding agent and may be bought from Indian and Pakistani grocery stores.*

Strained Dhal with Meatballs

This is a dhal *with a difference. After cooking it, put meatballs (koftas) in it and a few fried potato wafers. Serve it with fried spicy rice (see page 160) or plain boiled rice and poppadoms.*

Serves 6–8

INGREDIENTS

1¹/₂ cups *masoor dhal*
1 tsp crushed fresh ginger root
1 tsp crushed garlic
¹/₂ tsp turmeric
1¹/₂ tsp chili powder
1¹/₂ tsp salt
3 tbsp lemon juice
3³/₄ cups water

TO GARNISH:
3 fresh green chilies, finely chopped
fresh cilantro leaves, chopped

BAGHAAR:
²/₃ cup oil
3 garlic cloves
4 dried red chilies

1 tsp white cumin seeds

POTATO FRIES:
pinch of salt
2 medium potatoes, sliced thinly
1¹/₄ cups oil

1 Rinse the lentils, removing any stones.

2 Place the lentils in a saucepan and cover with 2¹/₂ cups water. Add the ginger, garlic, turmeric, and chili powder and boil until the lentils are soft and mushy. Add the salt, stirring.

3 Mash the lentils, then push them through a strainer, reserving the liquid. Add the lemon juice to the strained liquid.

4 Stir 1¹/₄ cups of the water into the strained liquid and bring to a boil over a low heat. Set aside.

5 To make the meatballs, follow the recipe for beef kabobs on page 46—use the reserved strained lentil liquid instead of water, and shape into small balls rather than into flat patties. Drop the meatballs gently into the lentil mixture.

6 Prepare the *baghaar*. Heat the oil in a pan. Add the garlic,

dried red chilies, and white cumin seeds and fry for 2 minutes. Pour the *baghaar* over the lentil mixture, stirring to mix.

7 For the potato fries, rub the salt over the potato slices. Heat the oil in a skillet and fry the potatoes, turning occasionally, until crisp.

8 Garnish the meatballs with the fried potatoes, fresh green chilies, and cilantro.

Spiced Rice & Lentils

This is a lovely combination of rice and masoor dhal, *simple to cook and delicious served with ground lamb and chutney. When you serve this, add a pat of sweet butter.*

Serves 4

INGREDIENTS

1 cup basmati rice
¾ cup *masoor dhal*
2 tbsp pure or vegetable ghee

1 small onion, sliced
1 tsp finely chopped fresh
　ginger root

1 tsp crushed garlic
½ tsp turmeric
2½ cups water
1 tsp salt

1 Combine the rice and *dhal* and rinse twice, rubbing with your fingers, and remove any stones. Set aside until required.

2 Heat the ghee in a large saucepan. Add the onion and sauté for about 2 minutes.

3 Reduce the heat, add the ginger, garlic, and turmeric and stir-fry for 1 minute.

4 Add the rice and *dhal* to the mixture in the pan and blend together, mixing gently.

5 Add the water to the mixture in the pan and bring to a boil. Reduce the heat and cook, covered, for 20–25 minutes.

6 Just before serving, add the salt and mix to combine.

7 Transfer the spiced rice and lentils to a serving dish and serve immediately.

VARIATION

Moong dhal *may be substituted for* masoor dhal *in this recipe.*

COOK'S TIP

Many Indian recipes specify using ghee as the cooking fat. This is because it is similar to clarified butter in that it can be heated to a very high temperature without burning. Ghee adds a nutty flavor to dishes and a glossy shine to sauces. You can buy ghee in cans, and a vegetarian version is also available. Store at room temperature or keep in the refrigerator.

Chana Dhal Cooked with Rice

Saffron makes this dish rather special. It is delicious served with any raita (see page 216) and a meat curry, such as spicy lamb curry (see page 40).

Serves 6

INGREDIENTS

¾ cup *chana dhal*
4 tbsp ghee
2 medium onions, sliced
1 tsp finely chopped fresh
   ginger root
1 tsp crushed garlic
½ tsp turmeric

2 tsp salt
½ tsp chili powder
1 tsp garam masala
5 tbsp unsweetened yogurt
5⅔ cups water
⅔ cup milk
1 tsp saffron

3 tbsp lemon juice
2 fresh green chilies
fresh cilantro leaves
3 black cardamoms
3 black cumin seeds
2¼ cups basmati rice

1 Rinse and soak the *chana dhal* for 3 hours. Rinse the rice, remove any stones, and set aside.

2 Heat the ghee in a skillet. Add the onion and sauté until golden brown. Using a slotted spoon, remove half the onion with a little of the ghee and set aside in a bowl.

3 Add the ginger, garlic, turmeric, 1 tsp of the salt, the chili powder, and garam masala to the onion remaining in the pan and stir-fry for 5 minutes. Stir in the yogurt and add the *chana dhal* and ⅔ cup water. Cook, covered, for 15 minutes. Set aside.

4 Meanwhile, boil the milk with the saffron and set aside with the reserved fried onion, lemon juice, fresh green chilies, and cilantro leaves.

5 Boil the rest of the water and add the salt, black cardamoms, black cumin seeds, and the rice, and cook, stirring, until the rice is half-cooked. Drain, and place half the fried onion, saffron, lemon juice, fresh green chilies, and cilantro on top of the *chana dhal* mixture. Place the remaining rice on top of this, and the rest of the fried onion, saffron, lemon juice, chilies, and cilantro on top of the rice. Cover tightly with a lid and cook for 20 minutes over a very low heat. Mix with a slotted spoon before serving.

Pulao Rice

Plain boiled rice is eaten by most people in India every day, but for entertaining choose a more interesting rice dish, such as this one which has different-colored grains and spices in it.

Serves 2–4

INGREDIENTS

1 cup basmati rice
2 tbsp ghee
3 green cardamoms
2 cloves

3 peppercorns
1/2 tsp salt
1/2 tsp saffron

2 cups water

1 Rinse the rice twice and set aside until required.

2 Heat the ghee in a saucepan. Add the cardamoms, cloves, and peppercorns to the pan and fry, stirring, for about 1 minute.

3 Add the rice and stir-fry for a further 2 minutes.

4 Add the salt, saffron, and water to the rice mixture and reduce the heat. Cover the pan and simmer over a low heat until all the water has been absorbed.

5 Transfer to a serving dish and serve hot.

COOK'S TIP

The most expensive of all spices, saffron strands are the stamens of a type of crocus. They give dishes a rich, golden color, as well as adding a distinctive, slightly bitter taste. Saffron is sold as a powder or in strands. Saffron strands are more expensive, but do have a superior flavor. Some books recommend substituting turmeric—although the colors are similar, the tastes are not.

COOK'S TIP

Cloves should be used with caution because the flavor can be overwhelming if too many are used.

Fried Spicy Rice

*Ginger and garlic in this beautifully aromatic rice dish give it a
lovely flavor. If desired, you can add a few peas to it for extra color and variety.*

Serves 4–6

INGREDIENTS

2¼ cups rice
1 medium onion
2 tbsp ghee
1 tsp finely chopped fresh
  ginger root

1 tsp crushed garlic
1 tsp salt
1 tsp black cumin seeds
3 whole cloves

3 whole green cardamoms
2 cinnamon sticks
4 peppercorns
3¼ cups water

1 Rinse the rice, removing any stones.

2 Using a sharp knife, cut the onion into slices.

3 Melt the ghee in a large saucepan and sauté the onion until crisp and golden brown.

4 Add the ginger, garlic, and salt to the onion in the pan, stirring to combine.

5 With a slotted spoon, remove half the spicy onions from the saucepan and set aside.

6 Add the rice, black cumin seeds, cloves, cardamoms, cinnamon sticks, and peppercorns to the mixture in the pan and stir-fry for 3–5 minutes.

7 Add the water to the mixture in the pan and bring to a boil. Reduce the heat, cover, and cook until steam comes out through the lid. Check to see whether the rice is cooked.

8 Transfer the fried spicy rice to a serving dish and serve garnished with the reserved fried onions.

COOK'S TIP

Cardamom pods contain numerous tiny black seeds which have a warm flavor and are highly aromatic—green cardamoms are considered the best because of their fine delicate flavor. Green cardamoms are also prized for their digestive properties, and some Indians chew them raw after they have eaten extra-spicy curries, to aid digestion and sweeten the breath.

Vegetable Pulao

This is a lovely way of cooking rice and vegetables together, and the saffron gives it a beautiful aroma. Serve this with a raita (see page 216) and any kabob dish.

Serves 4–6

INGREDIENTS

2 medium potatoes, each peeled and cut into 6
1 medium eggplant, cut into 6
7 ounces carrots, peeled and sliced
1/4 cup sliced green beans
4 tbsp ghee
2 medium onions, sliced
3/4 cup unsweetened yogurt
2 tsp finely chopped fresh ginger root
2 tsp crushed garlic

2 tsp garam masala
2 tsp black cumin seeds
1/2 tsp turmeric
3 black cardamoms
2 cinnamon sticks
2 tsp salt
1 tsp chili powder
3 cups basmati rice
5 tbsp lemon juice
1/2 tsp saffron strands, boiled in 1 1/4 cups milk

TO GARNISH:
4 fresh green chilies, chopped
fresh cilantro leaves, chopped

1 Prepare the vegetables. Heat the ghee in a skillet and fry the potatoes, eggplant, carrots, and beans, turning. Remove from the skillet and set aside. Fry the onions until soft and add the yogurt, ginger, garlic, garam masala, 1 tsp black cumin seeds, turmeric, 1 cardamom, 1 cinnamon stick, 1 tsp salt, and the chili powder and stir-fry for 3–5 minutes. Return the vegetables to the pan and fry for 4–5 minutes.

2 In a pan of boiling water, half-cook the rice with 1 tsp salt, 2 cinnamon sticks, 2 black cardamoms, and 1 tsp black cumin seeds. Drain the rice, leaving half in the pan while transferring the other half to a bowl. Pour the vegetable mixture on top of the rice in the pan. Pour half of the lemon juice and half of the saffron in milk over the vegetables and rice, cover with the remaining rice, and pour the remaining lemon juice and saffron in milk over the top. Garnish with fresh green chilies and cilantro, return to the heat, and cover. Cook over a low heat for about 20 minutes. Serve hot.

Brown Rice with Fruit & Nuts

Here is a tasty and filling rice dish that is nice and spicy and includes fruits
for a refreshing flavor and toasted nuts for an interesting crunchy texture.

Serves 4–6

INGREDIENTS

4 tbsp vegetable ghee or oil
1 large onion, chopped
2 garlic cloves, crushed
1-inch piece fresh ginger root, finely chopped
1 tsp chili powder
1 tsp cumin seeds

1 tbsp mild or medium curry powder or paste
1^1/$_2$ cups brown rice
3^1/$_2$ cups boiling vegetable stock
14 ounce can chopped tomatoes
^{3}/$_4$ cup no-need-to-soak dried apricots or peaches, cut into slivers

1 red bell pepper, cored, seeded, and diced
^{3}/$_4$ cup frozen peas
1–2 small, slightly green bananas
^{1}/$_3$–^{1}/$_2$ cup toasted mixed nuts
salt and pepper

1 Heat the ghee or oil in a large saucepan, add the onion, and sauté gently for 3 minutes.

2 Stir in the garlic, ginger, chili powder, cumin seeds, curry powder or paste, and rice. Cook gently for 2 minutes, stirring all the time, until the rice is coated in the spiced oil.

3 Pour in the boiling stock, stirring to mix. Add the

tomatoes and season with salt and pepper to taste. Bring the mixture to a boil, then reduce the heat, cover the pan, and simmer gently for 40 minutes, or until the rice is almost cooked and most of the liquid is absorbed.

4 Add the apricots or peaches, red bell pepper, and peas to the rice mixture in the pan. Cover and continue cooking for 10 minutes.

5 Remove the pan from the heat and let stand for 5 minutes without uncovering.

6 Peel and slice the bananas. Uncover the rice mixture and toss with a fork to mix. Add the toasted nuts and sliced bananas and toss lightly.

7 Transfer the brown rice and fruit and nuts to a serving platter and serve hot.

Shrimp Pulao

This recipe features caraway seeds, which give a distinctive taste and aroma to this unusual shrimp pulao. Serve with a raita (see page 216) and beef kabobs (see page 46).

Serves 4

INGREDIENTS

1 pound frozen shrimp
1/2 tsp saffron
1 1/4 cups milk
1 tsp chili powder
1 1/2 tsp caraway seeds
2 cinnamon sticks

2 green cardamoms
1 tsp salt
2 medium onions, sliced
2 bay leaves
1 tsp finely chopped fresh
  ginger root

2 1/4 cups basmati rice
5 tbsp ghee
4 tbsp lemon juice
fresh mint leaves

1 Thaw the shrimp thoroughly by placing them in a bowl of cold water.

2 Prepare the saffron by boiling 2/3 cup of the milk in a pan and adding the saffron. Set aside until required.

3 Place the chili powder, 1 tsp caraway seeds, cinnamon sticks, green cardamoms, salt, 1 sliced onion, the bay leaves, and ginger in a mortar and grind to a fine paste with a pestle. Set aside.

4 Place the rice in a saucepan of boiling water and when the rice is half-cooked, remove from the heat and set aside.

5 Heat the ghee in a pan and sauté the remaining onion until golden brown. Transfer the onion to a bowl and mix with the lemon juice and mint leaves to taste.

6 Add the spice paste and shrimp to the pan and stir-fry for about 5 minutes. Remove the shrimps and spices and place in a bowl.

7 Place the half-cooked rice in a saucepan and pour the shrimp mixture on top. Pour half the onion and lemon mixture and half the saffron mixture over the shrimp. Place the other half of the rice on top and pour on the remaining ingredients.

8 Add extra mint leaves to taste, cover, and cook over a low heat for 15–20 minutes.

9 Mix well before transferring to a warm serving dish and serve immediately.

Chicken Biryani

This biryani *recipe may look rather complicated, but is not difficult to follow. You can substitute lamb for chicken, if desired, but you would have to marinate it overnight.*

Serves 6

INGREDIENTS

1¹/₂ tsp finely chopped fresh
   ginger root
1¹/₂ tsp crushed garlic
1 tbsp garam masala
1 tsp chili powder
¹/₂ tsp turmeric
2 tsp salt
20 crushed green/white cardamom
   seeds

1¹/₄ cups unsweetened yogurt
3 pound 5 ounces skinless chicken,
   cut into 8 pieces
²/₃ cup milk
saffron strands
6 tbsp ghee
2 medium onions, sliced
2¹/₄ cups basmati rice
2 cinnamon sticks

4 black peppercorns
1 tsp black cumin seeds
4 fresh green chilies, finely chopped
fresh cilantro leaves, finely chopped
4 tbsp lemon juice

1 Blend together the ginger, garlic, garam masala, chili powder, turmeric, 1 tsp salt, and cardamom seeds and mix with the yogurt and chicken pieces. Set aside to marinate for 3 hours.

2 Boil the milk in a pan, pour it over the saffron, and set aside.

3 Heat the ghee in a pan and sauté the onions until golden brown. Remove half the onions and ghee from the saucepan and set aside.

4 Place the rice in a pan. Add twice as much water, the cinnamon sticks, peppercorns, and the cumin seeds. Bring the rice to a boil and remove from the heat when half-cooked. Drain and place in a bowl. Mix with the remaining salt.

5 Add the chicken mixture to the pan containing the onion and ghee. Add half each of the chopped chilies, cilantro, lemon juice, and saffron. Add the rice and then the rest of the ingredients, including the reserved fried onions and ghee. Cover tightly so no steam escapes. Cook over a low heat for about 1 hour. Check that the meat is cooked right through before serving. If the meat is not cooked, return to the heat and cook for a further 15 minutes. Mix well before serving.

Tomato Rice

Rice cooked with tomatoes and onions will add color to your table, especially when garnished with fresh green chilies, cilantro leaves, and hard-boiled eggs.

Serves 4

INGREDIENTS

$^2/_3$ cup oil
2 medium onions, sliced
1 tsp onion seeds
1 tsp finely chopped fresh
   ginger root
1 tsp crushed garlic

$^1/_2$ tsp turmeric
1 tsp chili powder
$1^1/_2$ tsp salt
14 ounce can tomatoes
$2^1/_4$ cups basmati rice
$2^1/_2$ cups water

TO GARNISH:
3 fresh green chilies,
   finely chopped
fresh cilantro leaves, chopped
3 hard-boiled eggs

1 Heat the oil in a saucepan and fry the onions until golden brown.

2 Add the onion seeds, ginger, garlic, turmeric, chili powder, and salt, stirring to combine.

3 Reduce the heat, add the tomatoes, and stir-fry for 10 minutes, breaking them up.

4 Add the rice to the tomato mixture, stirring gently, to coat the rice in the mixture.

5 Pour in the water, stirring to incorporate. Cover the pan and cook over a low heat until the water has been absorbed and the rice is cooked.

6 Transfer the tomato rice to a warm serving dish.

7 Garnish the tomato rice with the finely chopped fresh green chilies, fresh cilantro leaves and shelled, halved hard-boiled eggs. Serve the tomato rice immediately.

COOK'S TIP

Onion seeds are always used whole in Indian cooking. They are often used in pickles and sprinkled over the top of nan breads (see page 178). Ironically, onion seeds don't have anything to do with the vegetable, but they look similar to the plant's seed, hence the name.

Lamb Biryani

Cooked on festive occasions, especially for weddings, lamb biryani *is among the most popular dishes in India. The meat can be cooked in advance and added to the rice on the day of the party.*

Serves 4–6

INGREDIENTS

²/₃ cup milk
1 tsp saffron
5 tbsp ghee
3 medium onions, sliced
2 pound 5 ounces lean lamb, cubed
7 tbsp unsweetened yogurt
1¹/₂ tsp finely chopped fresh
   ginger root

1¹/₂ tsp crushed garlic
2 tsp garam masala
2 tsp salt
¹/₄ tsp turmeric
2¹/₂ cups water
2¹/₄ cups basmati rice
2 tsp black cumin seeds
3 cardamoms

4 tbsp lemon juice
2 fresh green chilies
¹/₄ bunch fresh cilantro leaves

1 Boil the milk in a pan with the saffron and set aside. Heat the ghee in a pan and sauté the onions until golden. Remove half the onions and ghee from the pan and set aside in a bowl.

2 Combine the meat, yogurt, ginger, garlic, garam masala, 1 tsp salt, and the turmeric in a large bowl and mix well.

3 Return the pan with the ghee and onions to the heat, add the meat mixture, stir for about 3 minutes, and add the water. Cook over a low heat for 45 minutes, stirring occasionally. Check to see whether the meat is tender: if not, add ²/₃ cup water and cook for 15 minutes. Once all the water has evaporated, stir-fry for about 2 minutes and set aside.

4 Meanwhile, place the rice in a pan. Add the cumin seeds, cardamoms, salt, and enough water for cooking, and cook over a medium heat until the rice is half-cooked. Drain. Remove half the rice and place in a bowl.

5 Spoon the meat mixture on top of the rice in the pan. Add half each of the saffron mixture, lemon juice, chilies, and cilantro. Add the reserved onions and ghee, and the other half of the rice, saffron, lemon juice, chilies, and cilantro. Cover and cook over a low heat for 15–20 minutes, or until the rice is cooked. Stir well and serve.

Paratas Stuffed with Vegetables

*This bread can be quite rich and is usually made for special occasions.
It can be eaten on its own or with any meat or vegetable curry.*

Makes 4–6

INGREDIENTS

DOUGH:
1³/4 cups whole-wheat flour (*ata* or
   chapati flour)
¹/2 tsp salt
³/4 cup water
8 tbsp pure or vegetable ghee
2 tbsp ghee, for frying

FILLING:
3 medium potatoes
¹/2 tsp turmeric
1 tsp garam masala
1 tsp finely chopped fresh
   ginger root
fresh cilantro leaves

3 fresh green chilies, finely chopped
1 tsp salt

1 To make the *paratas*, mix the flour, salt, water, and ghee in a bowl to form a dough.

2 Divide the dough into 6–8 equal portions. Roll each portion out on a lightly floured counter. Brush the middle of the dough portions with ¹/2 tsp ghee. Fold the dough portions in half, roll into a pipe-like shape, flatten with the palms of your hands, then roll around your finger to form a coil. Roll out again, dusting with additional flour when necessary, to form a patty about 7 inches in diameter.

3 Place the potatoes in a saucepan of water and cook until soft enough to be mashed.

4 Blend the turmeric, garam masala, ginger, cilantro, chilies, and salt together in a bowl.

5 Add the spice mixture to the mashed potato and mix well. Spread about 1 tbsp of the spicy potato mixture on each dough portion and cover with another rolled-out piece of dough. Seal the edges well.

6 Heat 2 tsp ghee in a heavy-based skillet. Place the *paratas* gently in the skillet in batches and fry, adding more oil as needed, turning and moving them about gently with a flat spoon, until golden.

7 Remove the *paratas* from the skillet and serve immediately.

Gram Flour Bread

This filling bread is not eaten on a regular basis, but is best served with the white radish curry (see page 110), but goes well with any vegetarian curry and lime pickle.

Makes 4–6

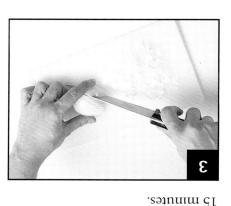

INGREDIENTS

3/4 cup whole-wheat flour (ata or chapati flour)	1 small onion finely chopped	2 fresh green chilies, very finely chopped
1/2 cup gram flour	fresh cilantro leaves, very finely chopped	2/3 cup water
1/2 tsp salt		2 tsp ghee

1 Sift the whole-wheat and gram flours together into a large mixing bowl.

2 Add the salt to the flour and mix to combine.

3 Using a sharp knife, chop the onion very finely.

4 Blend the onion, chopped cilantro, and chopped green chilies into the flour mixture.

5 Add the water and mix to form a soft dough. Cover and set aside for about 15 minutes.

6 Uncover the dough and knead thoroughly for 5–7 minutes.

7 Divide the dough into 8 equal portions.

8 Roll out the dough portions to about 7 inches on a lightly floured surface.

9 Place the dough portions individually in a skillet and cook over a medium heat, turning three times and lightly greasing each side with the ghee each time. Transfer the gram flour bread to serving plates and serve hot.

COOK'S TIP

Also called besan flour, gram flour is a pale yellow flour made from ground garbanzo beans. In Indian kitchens it is used to make breads, bhajis, and batters and to thicken sauces and stabilize yogurt when it is added to hot dishes. Buy it from Indian grocery stores or large healthfood stores and store in a cool, dark place in an airtight container.

Nan Bread

There are many ways of making nan bread, but this particular recipe is very easy to follow.
Nan bread should be served warm, preferably immediately after cooking.

Makes 6–8

1 tsp sugar	1½ cups all-purpose flour	6 tbsp sweet butter
1 tsp fresh yeast	1 tbsp ghee	1 tsp poppy seeds
⅔ cup warm water	1 tsp salt	

1 Put the sugar and yeast in a small bowl or pitcher with the warm water and mix well until the yeast has dissolved. Set aside for about 10 minutes, or until the mixture is frothy.

2 Place the flour in a large mixing bowl. Make a well in the middle of the flour, add the ghee and salt, and pour in the yeast mixture. Mix well to form a dough, using your hands and adding more water if required.

3 Turn the dough out onto a floured surface and knead for about 5 minutes, or until smooth.

4 Return the dough to the bowl, cover, and leave to rise in a warm place for 1½ hours, or until doubled in size.

5 Turn the dough out onto a floured surface and knead for a further 2 minutes. Break off small balls with your hand and pat them into rounds about 5 inches in diameter and ½ inch thick.

6 Place the dough rounds on a greased sheet of foil and broil under a very hot preheated broiler for 7–10 minutes, turning twice and brushing with the butter and sprinkling with the poppy seeds.

7 Serve warm immediately, or keep wrapped in foil until required.

COOK'S TIP

A tandoor oven throws out a ferocious heat; this bread is traditionally cooked on the side wall of the oven where the heat is only slightly less than in the center. For an authentic effect, leave your broiler on for a long time to heat up before the first dough goes under.

Chapati

This Indian bread contains no fat, but some people like to brush it with a little melted butter before serving.

Makes 10–12

INGREDIENTS

1¹/₂ cups whole-wheat flour (*ata* or *chapati* flour)

¹/₂ tsp salt

³/₄ cup water

1 Place the flour in a large mixing bowl. Add the salt and mix to combine.

2 Make a well in the middle of the flour and gradually pour in the water, mixing well with your fingers to form a supple dough.

3 Knead the dough for about 7–10 minutes. Ideally, set the dough aside and let it rise for 15–20 minutes, but if time is short, roll out the dough right away. Divide the dough into 10–12 equal portions. Roll out each piece of dough on a well-floured surface.

4 Place a heavy-based skillet on a high heat. When steam starts to rise from the skillet, lower the heat to medium.

5 Place a chapati in the skillet and when the chapati starts to bubble, turn it over. Carefully press down on the chapati with a clean dishcloth or a flat spoon and turn the chapati over once again. Remove the chapati from the skillet, set aside, and keep warm while you make the others.

6 Repeat the process until all the chapatis are cooked.

COOK'S TIP

Ideally, chapatis should be eaten as they come out of the skillet, but if that is not practical, keep them warm after cooking by wrapping them in foil. In India, chapatis are sometimes cooked on a naked flame, which makes them puff up. Allow about 2 per person.

Lightly Fried Bread

This is a rather rich bread, made only occasionally. Served with egg curry (see page 126) or ground almonds in ghee and milk (see page 250), it is delicious. Allow 2 breads per person.

Makes 10

INGREDIENTS

1^1/$_2$ cups whole-wheat flour (*ata* or *chapati* flour)

^{1}/$_2$ tsp salt
1 tbsp ghee

1^1/$_4$ cups water

1 Place the whole-wheat flour and the salt in a large bowl and mix to combine.

2 Make a well in the middle of the flour. Add the ghee and rub in well. Gradually pour in the water and work to form a soft dough. Set the dough aside to rise for 10–15 minutes.

3 Carefully knead the dough for 5–7 minutes then divide into about 10 equal portions.

4 On a lightly floured surface, roll out each dough portion to form a flat pancake shape.

5 Using a sharp knife, lightly draw lines in a crisscross pattern on each dough portion.

6 Heat a heavy-based skillet. Gently place the dough portions, one by one, into the pan.

7 Cook the bread for about 1 minute, then turn over and spread with 1 tsp ghee. Turn the bread over again and fry gently, moving it around the skillet with a spatula, until golden. Turn the bread over once again, then remove from the skillet and keep warm while you cook the remaining batches.

COOK'S TIP

In India, breads are cooked on a tava, *a traditional flat griddle. A large, heavy-based skillet makes an adequate substitute.*

Poori

This bread is served mostly with vegetarian meals and particularly with potato curry (see page 116) and cream of wheat dessert (see page 244). Although pooris are deep-fried, they are very light.

Makes 10

INGREDIENTS

1¹/₂ cups whole-wheat flour (*ata* or *chapati* flour)

¹/₂ tsp salt
²/₃ cup water

2¹/₂ cups oil

1 Place the flour and salt in a large mixing bowl and stir to combine.

2 Make a well in the center of the flour. Gradually pour in the water and mix together to form a dough, adding more water if necessary.

3 Knead the dough until it is smooth and elastic, and set aside in a warm place to rise for about 15 minutes.

4 Divide the dough into about 10 equal portions and with lightly oiled or floured hands pat each into a smooth ball.

5 On a lightly oiled or floured surface, roll out each ball to form a thin round.

6 Heat the oil in a deep skillet. Deep-fry the rounds in batches, turning once, until golden in color.

7 Remove the *pooris* from the skillet and drain. Serve hot.

COOK'S TIP

You can serve pooris either piled one on top of the other or spread out in a layer on a large serving platter so that they remain puffed up.

COOK'S TIP

You can make pooris in advance, if you prefer. Wrap in aluminum foil and reheat in a hot oven for about 10 minutes when required.

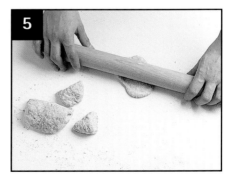

Snacks & Side Dishes

In India, tea parties are held at
about 5 or 6 o'clock in the evening, especially in
the month of Ramadan, when people meet after fasting
all day, and serve little snacks such as the ones in this
chapter. They are ideal for cocktail parties, when you
would like to offer something more interesting than the
usual peanuts and potato chips. The basic quantities
are for four people, but you can multiply according to
the number on your guest list.

Accompaniments—a simple Carrot
Salad or a Mint Raita, for example—always
add color and variety to a meal. Most take very
little time to prepare, but taste delicious. None of these
accompaniments has to be made in large quantities,
because they are taken only in small amounts:
variety is better than quantity!

Fried Eggplant in Yogurt

*This makes a good alternative to a raita. The eggplant
is fried until crisp, then given a* baghaar, *or seasoned-oil dressing.*

Serves 4

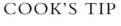

³/₄ cup unsweetened yogurt	1 medium eggplant	6 dried red chilies
¹/₃ cup water	²/₃ cup oil	
1 tsp salt	1 tsp white cumin seeds	

1 Place the yogurt in a bowl and beat with a fork.

2 Add the water and salt to the yogurt and mix well. Transfer to a serving bowl.

3 Using a sharp knife, slice the eggplant thinly.

4 Heat the oil in a large, heavy-based skillet. Add the eggplant slices and fry, in batches, over a medium heat, turning occasionally, until they begin to turn crisp. Remove from the skillet, transfer to a serving plate, and keep warm.

5 When all the eggplant slices have been fried, lower the heat, and add the white cumin seeds and the dried red chilies to the skillet. Cook for 1 minute, stirring constantly.

6 Spoon the yogurt on top of the eggplant, then pour the white cumin and red chili mixture on the eggplant. Serve immediately.

VARIATION

Finely chop and seed the dried red chilies, if desired.

COOK'S TIP

Rich in protein and calcium, yogurt plays an important part in Indian cooking. It is used as a marinade, as a creamy flavoring in curries and sauces, and as a cooling accompaniment to hot dishes.

Spicy Corn

This dish is an ideal accompaniment to a wide range of Indian meals.

Serves 4

INGREDIENTS

1 cup canned or frozen corn
1 tsp ground cumin
1 tsp fresh garlic, crushed

1 tsp ground coriander
1 tsp salt
2 fresh green chilies
1 medium onion, finely chopped

3 tbsp sweet butter
4 dried red chilies, crushed
$1/2$ tsp lemon juice
fresh cilantro leaves

1 Thaw frozen corn or drain canned corn and set aside.

2 Place the ground cumin, garlic, ground coriander, salt, 1 fresh green chili, and the onion in a mortar and grind with a pestle to form a smooth paste. Alternatively, process in a food processor to a smooth paste.

3 Heat the butter in a large, heavy-based skillet. Add the onion and spice mixture to the skillet and fry over a medium heat, stirring occasionally, for about 5–7 minutes.

4 Add the crushed red chilies to the skillet and stir to mix.

5 Add the corn to the skillet and stir-fry for a further 2 minutes.

6 Add the remaining fresh green chili, the lemon juice, and fresh cilantro leaves to the skillet, stirring occasionally to combine thoroughly.

7 Transfer the spicy corn mixture to a warm serving dish. Garnish with fresh cilantro and serve hot.

COOK'S TIP

Coriander is available ground or as seeds and is one of the essential ingredients in Indian cooking. Coriander seeds are often dry roasted before use to develop their flavor.

Pakoras

Pakoras are eaten all over India. They are made in many different ways and with a variety of fillings. Sometimes they are served in yogurt.

Serves 4

INGREDIENTS

6 tbsp gram flour
$1/2$ tsp salt
1 tsp chili powder
1 tsp baking powder
$1^1/2$ tsp white cumin seeds

1 tsp pomegranate seeds
$1^1/4$ cups water
fresh cilantro leaves, finely chopped

vegetables of your choice:
    cauliflower, cut into small florets;
    onions, cut into rings; potatoes,
    sliced; eggplants, slice; or fresh
    spinach leaves
oil, for deep-frying

1 Sift the gram flour into a large mixing bowl.

2 Add the salt, chili powder, baking powder, cumin, and pomegranate seeds and mix well.

3 Pour in the water and beat well to form a smooth batter.

4 Add the cilantro and mix. Set the batter aside.

5 Dip the prepared vegetables of your choice into the batter, shaking off any excess batter.

6 Heat the oil in a large heavy-based pan. Place the dipped vegetables in the oil and deep-fry, in batches, turning once.

7 Repeat this process until all the batter has been used up.

8 Transfer the vegetables to paper towels and drain thoroughly. Transfer to a serving dish and serve immediately.

COOK'S TIP

When deep-frying, it is important to use oil at the correct temperature. If the oil is too hot, the outside of the food will burn, as will the spices, before the inside is cooked. If the oil is too cool, the food will be sodden with oil before a crisp batter forms. Draining on paper towels is essential as it absorbs excess oil and moisture.

Indian-Style Omelet

Omelets go with almost anything and you can also serve them at any time of the day. For an informal lunch you could serve this omelet with French fries.

Serves 2–4

INGREDIENTS

1 small onion, very finely chopped
2 fresh green chilies, finely chopped

fresh cilantro leaves, finely chopped
4 medium eggs

1 tsp salt
2 tbsp oil

1 Place the onion, chilies, and cilantro in a large mixing bowl and mix together.

2 Place the eggs in a separate bowl and beat together.

3 Add the onion mixture to the eggs and mix together.

4 Add the salt to the egg and onion mixture and beat together well.

5 Heat 1 tbsp of the oil in a large, heavy-based skillet. Carefully place a ladleful of the omelet mixture into the skillet.

6 Cook the omelet, turning once and pressing down with a flat spoon to make sure that the egg is cooked right through, until the omelet is a golden brown color.

7 Repeat the same process for the remaining egg mixture. Set the omelets aside and keep warm while you make the remaining batches of omelets.

8 Serve the omelets immediately with paratas (see page 174) or toasted bread. Alternatively, simply serve the omelets with crisp salad greens for a light lunch.

COOK'S TIP

Indian cooks use a variety of vegetable oils, and peanut or sunflower oils make good alternatives for most dishes, although sometimes specific ones such as coconut oil, mustard oil, and sesame oil are called for.

Samosas

Samosas make excellent snacks. In India you can buy them along the roadside, and they are very popular. They are may be frozen and reheated.

Makes 10–12

INGREDIENTS

DOUGH:
3/4 cup self-rising flour
1/2 tsp salt
3 tbsp butter, cut into small pieces
4 tbsp water

FILLING:
3 medium potatoes, boiled
1 tsp finely chopped fresh
   ginger root
1 tsp crushed garlic
1/2 tsp white cumin seeds
1/2 tsp mixed onion and
   mustard seeds

1 tsp salt
1/2 tsp crushed dried red chilies
2 tbsp lemon juice
2 small fresh green chilies,
   finely chopped
ghee or oil, for deep-frying

1 Sift the flour and salt into a large mixing bowl. Add the butter and rub it into the flour until the mixture resembles fine bread crumbs.

2 Pour in the water and mix with a fork to form a dough. Pat the dough into a ball and knead for 5 minutes, or until the dough is smooth. Add a little flour if the dough is sticky. Cover and set aside to rise.

3 To make the filling, mash the boiled potatoes gently and mix with the ginger, garlic, white cumin seeds, onion and mustard seeds, salt, crushed red chilies, lemon juice, and green chilies.

4 Break small balls off the dough and roll each out very thinly to form a round. Cut in half, dampen the edges, and shape into cones. Fill the cones with a little of the filling, dampen the top and bottom edges, and pinch together to seal. Set aside.

5 Fill a deep pan one-third full with oil and heat until a small cube of bread browns in 30 seconds. Carefully lower the samosas into the oil, a few at a time, and fry for 2–3 minutes, or until golden brown. Remove from the oil and drain thoroughly on paper towels. Serve hot or cold.

Garbanzo Bean Snack

Although you may use fresh garbanzo beans, soaked overnight, for this popular snack eaten all over India, the canned beans are quick and easy to use without sacrificing flavor.

Serves 2–4

INGREDIENTS

14 ounce can garbanzo
  beans, drained
2 medium potatoes
1 medium onion
2 tbsp tamarind paste

6 tbsp water
1 tsp chili powder
2 tsp sugar
1 tsp salt

TO GARNISH:
1 tomato, sliced
2 fresh green chilies, chopped
fresh cilantro leaves

1 Place the drained garbanzo beans in a bowl.

2 Using a sharp knife, cut the potatoes into cubes.

3 Place the potatoes in a saucepan of water and boil until cooked through. Test by inserting the tip of a knife into the potatoes—they should feel soft and tender. Drain and set the potatoes aside until required.

4 Using a sharp knife, finely chop the onion. Set aside until required.

5 Mix together the tamarind paste and water in a small mixing bowl.

6 Add the chili powder, sugar, and salt to the tamarind paste mixture and mix together. Pour the mixture over the garbanzo beans.

7 Add the onion and the diced potatoes, and stir to mix. Season to taste with a little salt.

8 Transfer to a serving bowl and garnish with tomatoes, chilies, and cilantro leaves.

COOK'S TIP

Cream-colored and resembling a hazelnut in appearance, garbanzo beans have a nutty flavor and slightly crunchy texture. Indian cooks also grind these to make a flour called gram or besan, which is used to make breads, thicken sauces, and to make batters for deep-fried dishes.

Soft Dumplings in Yogurt with Masala

These are very light and make a good summer afternoon snack, as well as a good accompaniment to any vegetarian meal. They are usually served with their own special spice mixture in a small dish.

Serves 4

INGREDIENTS

1¹/₂ cups *urid dhal* powder
1 tsp baking powder
¹/₂ tsp ground ginger
1¹/₄ cups water
oil, for deep-frying
1¹/₂ cups unsweetened yogurt

5 tbsp sugar

MASALA:
6 tbsp ground coriander
6 tbsp ground white cumin
¹/₂ cup crushed dried red chilies

¹/₂ cup citric acid
chopped fresh red chilies, to garnish

1 Place the powdered *urid dhal* in a large mixing bowl. Add the baking powder and ground ginger and stir to combine. Add the water and mix to form a paste.

2 Heat the oil in a deep saucepan or skillet. Pour in the batter, 1 tsp at a time, and deep-fry the dumplings until golden brown, lowering the heat when the oil gets too hot. Set the dumplings aside.

3 Place the yogurt in a separate bowl. Add 1³/₄ cups water and the sugar and mix together with a whisk or fork. Set aside.

4 To make the *masala*, dry-fry the ground coriander and the white cumin in a saucepan until a little darker in color. Grind coarsely in a food processor, in a spice mill, or in a mortar with a pestle. Add the crushed dried red chilies and citric acid and blend well together.

5 Sprinkle about 1 tbsp of the *masala* over the dumplings and garnish with chopped fresh red chilies. Serve with the reserved yogurt mixture.

COOK'S TIP

The masala *(spice mixture) for the dumplings is usually made in a large quantity, as it can be stored in an airtight container.*

Spiced Cream of Wheat

A south Indian savory snack that is very quick and easy to prepare, this should be served warm. It has a lovely aroma, mainly from the curry leaves.

Serves 4

INGREDIENTS

2/3 cup oil
1 tsp mixed onion and mustard seeds
4 dried red chilies

4 curry leaves (fresh or dried)
8 tbsp coarse cream of wheat
1/3 cup cashews

1 tsp salt
2/3 cup water

1 Heat the oil in a large, heavy-based skillet.

2 Add the mixed onion and mustard seeds, dried red chilies, and curry leaves and stir-fry for about 1 minute, stirring constantly.

3 Reduce the heat and add the coarse cream of wheat and the cashews to the mixture in the skillet. Quickly stir-fry for about 5 minutes, moving the mixture around the skillet all the time so that it does not catch and burn on the base of the pan.

4 Add the salt to the mixture and continue to stir-fry, stirring constantly.

5 Add the water and cook, stirring continuously, until the mixture starts to thicken.

6 Serve the spiced cream of wheat warm as a snack.

COOK'S TIP

The basic quantity here is for 4 people, which you can multiply according to your guest list.

COOK'S TIP

Curry leaves are very similar in appearance to bay leaves but are very different in flavor. They can be bought both fresh and dried. They are mainly used to flavor lentil dishes and vegetable curries.

Sweet & Sour Fruit

This mixture of fresh and canned fruit, which has a sweet and sour flavor, is very cooling, especially in the summer. Serve tea or fruit juices with this.

Serves 4

INGREDIENTS

14 ounce can mixed fruit cocktail
14 ounce can guavas
2 large bananas

3 apples
1 tsp ground black pepper
1 tsp salt

2 tbsp lemon juice
$^{1}/_{2}$ tsp ground ginger
fresh mint leaves, to garnish

1 Drain the fruit cocktail and place the fruit in a deep mixing bowl.

2 Mix the guavas and their syrup with the drained fruit cocktail.

3 Peel the bananas and cut them into slices.

4 Peel, core, and dice the apples.

5 Add the fresh fruit to the bowl containing the canned fruit and mix together.

6 Add the ground black pepper, salt, lemon juice, and ginger and stir to mix.

7 Serve as a snack, garnished with a few fresh mint leaves.

COOK'S TIP

The lemon juice in this recipe serves to add a sharp flavor to the dish, but it also prevents the banana and apple from discoloring and turning brown when the flesh is exposed to the air.

COOK'S TIP

Ginger is one of the most popular spices in India and also one of the oldest. It can be bought as fresh ginger root in most large supermarkets. It should always be peeled before use and can be finely chopped or puréed. Ground ginger is also useful to have in your cupboard.

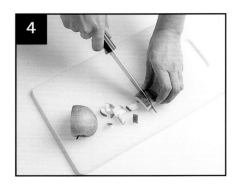

Mixed Rice, Nuts, & Raisins

This is one of the most popular nut mixtures in India and is very tasty. Make a large quantity and store it in an airtight container to serve with tea or cocktails.

Serves 4

INGREDIENTS

¹/₃ cup *chana dhal*
1¹/₄ cups oil
2 tsp onion seeds
6 curry leaves

3 cups *parva* (flaked rice)
2 tbsp peanuts
2 tbsp raisins
5 tbsp sugar

2 tsp salt
2 tsp chili powder
2 ounces *sev* (optional)

1 Rinse and soak the *chana dhal* in a bowl of water for at least 3 hours.

2 Heat the oil in a saucepan. Add the onion seeds and the curry leaves and fry, stirring constantly, until the onion seeds are crisp and golden.

3 Add the *parva* (flaked rice) to the mixture in the pan and fry until crisp and golden (do not allow to burn).

4 Remove the mixture from the pan and drain on paper towels so that any excess oil is soaked up.

5 Fry the peanuts in the remaining oil, stirring.

6 Add the peanuts to the flaked rice mixture, stirring to mix well.

7 Add the raisins, sugar, salt, and chili powder and mix together. Mix in the *sev* (if using). Transfer to a serving dish.

8 Reheat the oil remaining in the pan and fry the drained *chana dhal* until golden. Add to the other ingredients in the serving dish and mix together.

9 This dish can be eaten right away or stored in an airtight container until you need it.

COOK'S TIP

Sev are very thin sticks made of gram flour which can be bought in Indian and Pakistani grocery stores.

Deep-Fried Diamond Pastries

A simple-to-make snack that will retain its crispness if stored in an airtight container. Serve with drinks.

Serves 4

INGREDIENTS

1 cup all-purpose flour
1 tsp baking powder

$^1/_2$ tsp salt
1 tbsp black cumin seeds
$^1/_2$ cup water

$1^1/_4$ cups oil

1 Place the flour in a large mixing bowl.

2 Add the baking powder, salt, and the black cumin seeds and stir to mix.

3 Add the water to the dry ingredients and mix to form a soft, elastic dough.

4 Roll out the dough on a clean counter until it is about $^1/_4$ inch thick.

5 Using a sharp knife, cut the dough to form diamond shapes. Re-roll the trimmings and cut out more diamond shapes until all the dough has been used up.

6 Heat the oil in a large pan until a cube of bread browns in 30 seconds.

7 Carefully place the pastry diamonds in the oil, in batches if necessary, and deep-fry until golden brown.

8 Remove the diamond pastries with a slotted spoon and drain on paper towels. Serve with a *dhal* for dipping or store in an airtight container and serve when required.

COOK'S TIP

Black cumin seeds are used here for their strong aromatic flavor. White cumin seeds may not be used as a substitute.

Hot Salad

This quickly made dish is ideal for a cold winter's night.

Serves 4

INGREDIENTS

¹/₂ medium-size cauliflower	¹/₂ cucumber	salt and pepper
1 green bell pepper	4 carrots	
1 red bell pepper	2 tbsp butter	

1 Rinse the cauliflower and cut into small florets, using a sharp knife.

2 Seed the bell peppers and cut the flesh into thin slices.

3 Cut the cucumber into thin slices.

4 Peel the carrots and cut them into thin slices.

5 Melt the butter in a large saucepan, stirring constantly so that it doesn't burn.

6 Add the cauliflower, bell peppers, cucumber, and carrots and stir-fry for 5–7 minutes. Season with salt and pepper to taste, cover with a lid, reduce the heat, and leave to simmer for about 3 minutes.

7 Transfer the vegetables to a serving dish, toss to mix, and serve immediately.

COOK'S TIP

In India, you can buy snacks and accompaniments along the roadside, while elsewhere you can buy them from Indian or Pakistani grocery stores. However, they are fresher and more satisfying made at home.

VARIATION

You can replace the vegetables in this recipe with your favorites, if desired.

Cool Cucumber Salad

This cooling salad is another good foil for a highly spiced meal.
Omit the green chili, if desired.

Serves 4

INGREDIENTS

8 ounces cucumber
1 fresh green chili (optional)

fresh cilantro leaves, finely chopped
2 tbsp lemon juice
$^1/_2$ tsp salt

1 tsp sugar
fresh mint leaves, to garnish

1 Using a sharp knife, slice the cucumber thinly. Arrange the cucumber slices decoratively on a round serving plate.

2 Using a sharp knife, chop the green chili (if using).

3 Scatter the chopped chili over the cucumber.

4 To make the dressing, place the cilantro, lemon juice, salt, and sugar in a bowl, mix together, and set aside.

5 Chill the plate of cucumber in the refrigerator for a

minimum of 1 hour, or until required.

6 Remove the cucumber from the refrigerator. Pour the dressing over the cucumber just before serving and garnish with a few fresh mint leaves.

COOK'S TIP

To store fresh cilantro, put the roots in a glass of water and keep in a cool place for up to 4 days.

COOK'S TIP

Much of the heat in Indian dishes comes from the use of fresh green chilies, although dried and ground red chilies are also commonplace in Indian kitchens. In southern India, with its searingly hot temperatures, chilies are used in copious amounts because they cause the body to perspire, which has a cooling effect. Numerous varieties of fresh chili grow in India, from fairly mild to hot. As a general rule, the smaller the chili, the hotter it will be. Fresh chilies will keep for about 5 days in the refrigerator.

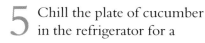

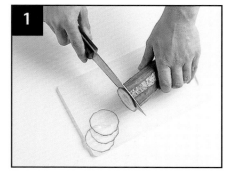

Garbanzo Bean Salad

This attractive salad can be served with a couple of beef kabobs
(see page 46) for a delicious light lunch or an informal supper.

Serves 4

INGREDIENTS

14 ounce can garbanzo beans	1 medium cucumber	1 red bell pepper, seeded
4 carrots	$^{1}/_{2}$ tsp salt	
1 bunch scallions	$^{1}/_{2}$ tsp pepper	
	3 tbsp lemon juice	

1 Drain the garbanzo beans and place them in a large salad bowl.

2 Using a sharp knife, peel and slice the carrots.

3 Using a sharp knife, cut the scallions into small pieces.

4 Cut the cucumber into thick quarters.

5 Add the carrots, scallions, and cucumber to the garbanzo beans and mix.

6 Season with the salt and pepper and sprinkle with the lemon juice.

7 Toss the salad ingredients together gently, using 2 serving spoons.

8 Using a sharp knife, slice the red bell pepper thinly.

9 Arrange the slices of red bell pepper on top of the garbanzo bean salad. Serve the salad immediately or chill in the refrigerator and serve when required.

COOK'S TIP

Using canned garbanzo beans rather than the dried ones speeds up the preparation time.

Raitas

Raitas are very easy to prepare, extremely versatile, and have a cooling effect that will be appreciated if you are serving hot, spicy dishes.

Serves 4

INGREDIENTS

MINT RAITA:
$3/4$ cup unsweetened yogurt
4 tbsp water
1 small onion, finely chopped
$1/2$ tsp mint sauce
$1/2$ tsp salt
3 fresh mint leaves, to garnish

CUCUMBER RAITA:
8 ounces cucumber
1 medium onion
$1/2$ tsp salt
$1/2$ tsp mint sauce
$1^1/4$ cups unsweetened yogurt
$2/3$ cup water
fresh mint leaves, to garnish

EGGPLANT RAITA:
1 medium eggplant
1 tsp salt
1 small onion, finely chopped
2 fresh green chilies, finely chopped
$3/4$ cup unsweetened yogurt
3 tbsp water

1 To make the mint raita, place the yogurt in a bowl and beat with a fork. Gradually add the water, beating well. Add the onion, mint sauce, and salt and blend together. Garnish with the fresh mint leaves.

2 To make the cucumber raita, peel and slice the cucumber. Using a sharp knife, chop the onion finely. Place the cucumber and onion in a large bowl, then add the salt and the mint sauce. Add the yogurt and the water and place the mixture in a blender and blend well. Transfer to a serving bowl and serve garnished with a few fresh mint leaves.

3 To make the eggplant raita, rinse the eggplant and remove the top end. Discard the top and chop the rest into small pieces. Boil the eggplant in a pan of water until soft and mushy. Drain the eggplant and mash. Transfer to a serving bowl and add the salt, the onion, and green chilies, mixing well. Beat the yogurt with the water in a separate bowl and pour over the eggplant mixture. Mix well and serve.

Mango Chutney

Everyone's favorite chutney, this has a sweet and sour taste and is particularly good served with a mint raita (see page 216). It is best made in advance and stored for at least two weeks before use.

Serves 4

INGREDIENTS

2¼ pounds raw mangoes	2 tsp finely chopped ginger root	½ cup raisins
4 tbsp salt	2 tsp garlic, crushed	½ cup dates, pitted
2½ cups water	2 tsp chili powder	
2⅓ cups sugar	2 cinnamon sticks	
2 cups vinegar		

1 Using a sharp knife, peel, halve, and pit the mangoes. Cut the mango flesh into cubes. Place the mangoes in a large bowl. Add the salt and water and leave overnight. Drain the liquid from the mangoes and set aside.

2 Bring the sugar and vinegar to a boil in a large saucepan over a low heat, stirring.

3 Gradually add the mango cubes to the sugar and vinegar mixture, stirring to coat the mango in the mixture.

4 Add the ginger, garlic, chili powder, cinnamon sticks, raisins, and dates, and bring to a boil again, stirring occasionally. Reduce the heat and cook for about 1 hour, or until the mixture thickens. Remove from the heat and cool.

5 Remove the cinnamon sticks and discard.

6 Spoon the chutney into clean dry jars and cover tightly with lids. Leave in a cool place for the flavors to develop fully.

COOK'S TIP

When choosing mangoes, select ones that are shiny with unblemished skins. To test if they are ripe, gently cup the mango in your hand and squeeze it lightly—it should give slightly to the touch if ready for eating.

Sesame Seed Chutney

This chutney goes nicely with spiced rice and lentils (see page 154).
Use it to spread in sandwiches, too.

Serves 4

INGREDIENTS

8 tbsp sesame seeds	3 fresh green chilies, chopped	1 medium onion, cut into rings
2 tbsp water	1 tsp salt	
1/2 bunch fresh cilantro	2 tsp lemon juice	

1 Place the sesame seeds in a large, heavy-based saucepan and dry-fry them.

2 Set the sesame seeds aside to cool.

3 Once cooled, place the sesame seeds in a food processor or in mortar and grind to form a fine powder.

4 Add the water to the sesame seeds and mix to a form a smooth paste.

5 Using a sharp knife, finely chop the cilantro.

6 Add the chilies and cilantro to the sesame seed paste and grind once again.

7 Add the salt and lemon juice to the mixture and grind once again.

8 Remove the mixture from the food processor or mortar and transfer to a serving dish. Garnish with the onion rings.

COOK'S TIP

Rinsing raw onions with water takes the edge off the raw taste.

COOK'S TIP

Dry-frying coaxes all of the flavor out of dried spices and gives dishes well-harmonized flavors that do not taste raw. Dry-frying takes only a few minutes and you will be able to tell when the spices are ready because of the wonderful fragrance that develops. Be sure to stir the spices constantly and never take your eyes off the pan because the spices can burn very quickly.

Tamarind Chutney

A mouth-watering chutney that is extremely popular all over India, served with various vegetarian snacks. Enjoy this with samosas (see page 196).

Serves 4–6

(see page 196)

INGREDIENTS

2 tbsp tamarind paste
5 tbsp water
1 tsp chili powder

1/2 tsp ground ginger
1/2 tsp salt
1 tsp sugar

finely chopped cilantro leaves,
to garnish

1 Place the tamarind paste in a mixing bowl.

2 Gradually add the water to the tamarind paste, gently beating with a fork to form a smooth, runny paste.

3 Add the chili powder and the ginger to the mixture and blend well.

4 Add the salt and the sugar and mix well.

5 Transfer the chutney to a serving dish and garnish with the cilantro.

COOK'S TIP

Vegetable dishes are often given a sharp, sour flavor with the addition of tamarind. This is made from the semi-dried, compressed pulp of the tamarind tree. You can buy bars of the pungent pulp in Indian and oriental grocery stores. Store it in a tightly sealed plastic bag or airtight container. Alternatively, for greater convenience, keep a jar of tamarind paste in your cupboard and use as required. Although tamarind is much stronger than lemon, lemon juice is often used as a substitute.

COOK'S TIP

Chili powder, or cayenne pepper, is a very fiery spice that should be used with caution.

Desserts

Indian meals usually end with something sweet, just as they do in the West. Indian desserts are quite rich and very sweet, so it is a good idea to offer a choice of fresh fruit—mangoes, guavas, or melon, for example—as well. These are best served chilled, especially in the summer months.

Desserts such as Indian Bread Pudding, Carrot Dessert, and Indian Vermicelli Dessert are served only for special occasions, such as a religious festival. This chapter also includes some simple desserts, such as Indian Rice Pudding, as well as the more elaborate desserts. Try some of these dishes. Because few restaurants offer much in the way of special Indian desserts they are usually a complete revelation to Western guests— and always a pleasant one!

Almond Slices

A mouth-watering dessert that is sure to impress your guests,
especially if served with whipped cream

Serves 6–8

INGREDIENTS

3 medium eggs
$^1/_2$ cup ground almonds
$1^1/_2$ cups milk powder

1 cup sugar
$^1/_2$ tsp saffron strands
8 tbsp sweet butter

1 tbsp flaked almonds

1 Beat the eggs together in a bowl and set aside.

2 Place the ground almonds, milk powder, sugar, and saffron in a large mixing bowl and stir to mix well.

3 Melt the butter in a small saucepan.

4 Pour the melted butter over the dry ingredients and mix well with a fork.

5 Add the reserved beaten eggs to the mixture and stir to blend well.

6 Carefully spread the cake mixture in a shallow 7–9-inch ovenproof dish and bake in a preheated oven at 325°F for 45 minutes. Test whether the cake is cooked by piercing with the tip of a knife or a toothpick—it will come out clean if the cake is cooked thoroughly.

7 Cut the almond cake mixture into slices.

8 Decorate the almond slices with flaked almonds and transfer to serving plates. Serve hot or cold.

COOK'S TIP

These almond slices are best eaten hot, but they may also be served cold. They can be made a day or even a week in advance and re-heated. They also freeze beautifully.

Sweet Potato Dessert

This milky dessert can be eaten hot or cold.

Serves 8–10

INGREDIENTS

2$\frac{1}{4}$ pounds sweet potatoes
3$\frac{1}{2}$ cups milk

1$\frac{3}{4}$ cups sugar

a few chopped almonds, to decorate

1 Using a sharp knife, peel the sweet potatoes. Rinse the sweet potatoes and cut them into slices.

2 Place the sweet potato slices in a large saucepan. Cover with 2$\frac{1}{2}$ cups milk and cook gently until the sweet potato is soft enough to be mashed.

3 Remove the sweet potatoes from the heat and mash to remove all the lumps.

4 Add the sugar and the remaining 1$\frac{1}{4}$ cups milk to the mashed sweet potatoes, and carefully stir to blend the mixture together.

5 Return the pan to the heat and simmer the mixture until it starts to thicken (it should reach the consistency of a cream of chicken soup).

6 Transfer the sweet potato dessert to a serving dish.

7 Decorate with the chopped almonds and serve.

COOK'S TIP

Sweet potatoes are longer than ordinary potatoes and have a pinkish or yellowish skin with yellow or white flesh. As their name suggests, they taste slightly sweet.

Deep-Fried Sweetmeat in Syrup

This is one of the most popular Indian sweetmeats. The flavor and beautiful aroma of this sweetmeat comes from rosewater. The finished dish can be served hot or cold.

Serves 6–8

INGREDIENTS

5 tbsp dried full cream milk powder
1¹/₂ tbsp all-purpose flour
1 tsp baking powder
1¹/₂ tbsp sweet butter
1 medium egg
1 tsp milk to mix (if required)

10 tbsp pure or vegetable ghee

SYRUP:
3¹/₄ cups water
8 tbsp sugar
2 green cardamoms, peeled, with
seeds crushed

1 large pinch saffron strands
2 tbsp rosewater

1 Place the dried full cream milk powder, flour, and baking powder in a bowl.

2 Place the butter in a pan and heat until melted, stirring.

3 Beat the egg in a bowl. Add the melted butter and beaten egg to the dry ingredients and blend together with a fork (and add the 1 tsp extra milk at this stage if necessary) to form a soft dough.

4 Break the dough into about 12 small pieces and shape, in the palms of your hands, into small, smooth balls.

5 Heat the ghee in a deep skillet. Reduce the heat and start frying the dough balls, about 3–4 at a time, tossing and turning gently with a slotted spoon until a dark golden brown color. Remove the sweetmeats from the pan and set aside in a deep serving bowl.

6 To make the syrup, boil the water and sugar in a pan for 7–10 minutes. Add the crushed cardamom seeds and saffron, and pour the syrup over the sweetmeats.

7 Pour the rosewater sparingly over the top. Let soak for about 10 minutes in order for the sweetmeats to soak up some of the syrup. Serve hot or cold.

Rice Pudding

We cook our rice pudding in a saucepan over a low heat rather than in the oven like the British version—which is also far less sweet. Rice pudding is one of the most popular of all desserts in India.

Serves 8–10

INGREDIENTS

¹/₄ cup basmati rice
5 cups milk

8 tbsp sugar

varq (silver leaf) or chopped
pistachios, to decorate

1 Rinse the rice and place in a large saucepan. Add 2¹/₂ cups of the milk and bring to a boil over a very low heat. Cook until the milk has been completely absorbed by the rice, stirring occasionally.

2 Remove the pan from the heat. Mash the rice, making swift, round movements in the pan, for at least 5 minutes until all the lumps have been removed.

3 Return the pan to the heat and gradually add the remaining 2¹/₂ cups milk. Bring to a boil over a low heat, stirring occasionally.

4 Add the sugar and continue to cook, stirring constantly, for 7–10 minutes, or until the mixture is quite thick in consistency.

5 Transfer the rice pudding to a heatproof serving bowl. Decorate with *varq* (silver leaf) or chopped pistachios and serve on its own or with pooris (see page 236).

VARIATION

If desired, you can substitute white or patna long grain rice for the basmati rice, but the result won't be as good.

COOK'S TIP

Varq is edible silver that is used to decorate elaborate dishes prepared for the most special occasions and celebrations, such as weddings, in India. It is pure silver that has been beaten until it is wafer thin. It comes with a piece of backing paper which is peeled off as the varq *is laid on the cooked food. It is extremely delicate and so must be handled with care. You can buy* varq *in Indian grocery stores, and remember that because it is pure silver, it should be stored in an airtight bag or box so that it doesn't tarnish.*

Pistachio Dessert

An attractive dessert, especially when decorated with varq, *this is another dish that can be prepared in advance. It is delicious served with cream.*

Serves 4–6

INGREDIENTS

3$^1/_2$ cups water	2$^1/_3$ cups sugar	TO DECORATE:
3 cups pistachios	2 cardamoms, with seeds crushed	$^1/_4$ cup flaked almonds
1$^3/_4$ cups full cream	2 tbsp rosewater	fresh mint leaves
dried milk	a few strands saffron	

1 Boil about 2$^1/_2$ cups water in a saucepan. Remove the pan from the heat and soak the pistachios in this water for about 5 minutes. Drain the pistachios thoroughly and remove the skins.

2 Grind the pistachios in a food processor or in a mortar with a pestle.

3 Add the dried milk powder to the ground pistachios and mix well.

4 To make the syrup, place the remaining 1$^1/_4$ cups water and the sugar in a pan and heat gently. When the liquid begins to thicken, add the cardamom seeds, rosewater, and saffron.

5 Add the syrup to the pistachio mixture and cook for about 5 minutes, stirring, until the mixture thickens. Set the mixture aside and cool slightly.

6 Once the mixture is cool enough to handle, roll it into balls (use up all the pistachio mixture). Decorate with the flaked almonds and fresh mint leaves and allow to set before serving.

COOK'S TIP

It is best to buy whole pistachios and grind them yourself, rather than using packets of ready ground nuts. Freshly ground nuts have the best flavor as grinding releases their natural oils.

Pooris Stuffed with Chana Dhal Halva

This is a very old recipe handed down to me by my mother. The pooris *freeze well so it pays to make a large quantity and reheat them in the oven.*

Makes 10

INGREDIENTS

POORIS:
1 cup coarse cream of wheat
3/4 cup all-purpose flour
1/2 tsp salt
1 1/2 tbsp ghee, plus extra for frying
2/3 cup milk

FILLING:
8 tbsp *chana dhal*
3 1/2 cups water
5 tbsp ghee
2 green cardamoms, peeled
4 cloves

8 tbsp sugar
2 tbsp ground almonds
1/2 tsp saffron strands
1/4 cup golden raisins

1 To make the *pooris*, place the cream of wheat, flour, and salt in a bowl and mix. Add the ghee and rub in with your fingers. Add the milk and mix to form a dough. Knead the dough for 5 minutes, cover, and allow to rise for about 3 hours. Knead the dough on a floured surface for 15 minutes.

2 Roll out the dough until it measures 10 inches and divide into ten portions. Roll out each of these into 5-inch rounds and set aside.

3 To make the filling, soak the *chana dhal* for at least 3 hours if time allows. Place the *dhal* in a pan and add 3 3/4 cups water. Bring to a boil over a medium heat until all of the water has evaporated and the *dhal* is soft enough to be mashed into a paste.

4 In a separate saucepan, heat the ghee and add the cardamom seeds and cloves. Reduce the heat, add the *chana dhal* paste, and stir for 5–7 minutes.

5 Fold in the sugar and almonds and cook, stirring, for 10 minutes. Add the saffron and golden raisins and blend until thickened, stirring, for 5 minutes.

6 Spoon the filling onto one half of each pastry round. Dampen the edges with water and fold the other half over to seal.

7 Heat the extra ghee in a pan and fry the filled *pooris* over a low heat until golden. Transfer to paper towels, drain, and serve.

Indian Bread Pudding

This, the Indian equivalent of the English bread and butter pudding, is rather
a special dessert, usually cooked for weddings or other special occasions.

Serves 4–6

INGREDIENTS

6 medium slices bread
5 tbsp ghee (preferably pure)
10 tbsp sugar
1¼ cups water
3 green cardamoms, without husks

2½ cups milk
¾ cup evaporated milk or *khoya* (see
   Cook's Tip)
½ tsp saffron strands

TO DECORATE:
8 pistachios, soaked, peeled,
   and chopped
chopped almonds
2 leaves *varq* (silver leaf) (optional)

1 Cut the bread slices into quarters.

2 Heat the ghee in a skillet and fry the bread slices, turning once, until crisp and golden brown in color.

3 Place the fried bread in the bottom of a heatproof dish and set aside.

4 To make a syrup, place the sugar, water, and cardamom seeds in a pan and bring to a boil until the syrup thickens.

5 Pour the syrup over the fried bread.

6 In a separate pan, bring the milk, evaporated milk or *khoya* (see Cook's Tip), and the saffron to a boil over a low heat until the milk has halved in volume.

7 Pour the milk over the syrup-coated bread.

8 Decorate with the pistachios, chopped almonds, and *varq* (if using). Serve the bread pudding with or without cream.

COOK'S TIP

To make khoya, *bring 3¾ cups milk to a boil in a large, heavy saucepan, watching the milk carefully so that it doesn't burn. Reduce the heat and boil for 35–40 minutes, stirring occasionally. The milk should reduce to a quarter of its volume, and when completely cooked should resemble a sticky dough.*

Almond Sherbet

*Use whole almonds rather than ready ground almonds
for this dish as they give it a better texture.*

Serves 2

INGREDIENTS

2 cups whole almonds
2 tbsp sugar

$1^1/_4$ cups milk

$1^1/_4$ cups water

1 Soak the almonds in a bowl of water for at least 3 hours or preferably overnight.

2 Using a sharp knife, chop the almonds into small pieces. Grind to a fine paste in a food processor or in a mortar.

3 Add the sugar to the almond paste and grind once again to form a fine paste.

4 Add the milk and water and mix well (in a blender if you have one).

5 Transfer the almond sherbet to a large serving dish.

6 Chill the almond sherbet in the refrigerator for about 30 minutes. Stir the almond sherbet just before serving.

COOK'S TIP

An electric coffee grinder or spice mill will greatly cut down the time taken to grind the almonds. If using a coffee grinder that is also used for coffee, always remember to clean the grinder afterwards, otherwise you will end up with strange-tasting coffee! A pestle and mortar will take longer and is not as good for large quantities.

COOK'S TIP

In India, ice cool sherbets such as this one are served on special occasions, such as religious festivals. They would be served on the very finest tableware and decorated with varq, the edible silver or gold leaf.

Coconut Candy

Quick and easy to make, this candy is very similar to coconut ice.
Pink food coloring may be added toward the end if desired.

Serves 4–6

INGREDIENTS

6 tbsp butter
3 cups shredded coconut
3/4 cup condensed milk

a few drops of pink food coloring
(optional)

1 Place the butter in a heavy-based saucepan and melt over a low heat, stirring so that the butter doesn't burn on the bottom of the pan.

2 Add the shredded coconut to the melted butter, stirring to mix thoroughly.

3 Stir in the condensed milk and the pink food coloring (if using) and mix continuously for 7–10 minutes.

4 Remove the saucepan from the heat, set aside, and leave the coconut mixture to cool slightly.

5 Once cool enough to handle, shape the coconut mixture into long blocks and cut into equal-size rectangles. Allow to set for about 1 hour, then serve.

COOK'S TIP

Coconut is used extensively in Indian cooking to add flavor and creaminess to various dishes. The best flavor comes from freshly grated coconut, although ready prepared shredded coconut, as used here, makes an excellent standby. Freshly grated coconut freezes successfully, so it is well worth preparing when you have the time.

VARIATION

If desired, you could divide the coconut mixture in step 2, and add the pink food coloring to only one half of the mixture. This way, you will have an attractive combination of pink and white coconut candies.

Cream of Wheat Dessert

This dish is eaten with pooris (see page 236) and potato curry (see page 116) for breakfast in northern India. If you like, you can serve it with fresh cream for a delicious dessert.

Serves 4

INGREDIENTS

6 tbsp pure ghee
3 whole cloves
3 whole cardamoms
8 tbsp coarse cream of wheat
$^1/_2$ tsp saffron

$^1/_2$ cup golden raisins
10 tbsp sugar
$1^1/_4$ cups water
$1^1/_4$ cups milk
cream, to serve

TO DECORATE:
$^1/_2$ cup shredded coconut, toasted
$^1/_4$ cup chopped almonds
$^1/_4$ cup pistachios, soaked and
chopped (optional)

1 Place the ghee in a saucepan and melt over a medium heat.

2 Add the cloves and the whole cardamoms to the melted butter and reduce the heat, stirring to mix.

3 Add the cream of wheat to the mixture in the pan and stir-fry until it turns a little darker.

4 Add the saffron, golden raisins, and the sugar to the cream of wheat mixture, stirring.

5 Pour in the water and milk and stir-fry the mixture continuously until the cream of wheat has softened. Add more water if required.

6 Remove the pan from the heat and transfer the cream of wheat to a serving dish.

7 Decorate the cream of wheat dessert with the toasted shredded coconut, flaked almonds, and pistachios. Serve with a little cream drizzled over the top.

COOK'S TIP

Cloves are used to give flavor and aroma to both sweet and savory dishes, but should be used with caution because the flavor can be overwhelming if too many are used.

Carrot Dessert

This makes a very impressive dinner party dessert. It is best served warm, with fresh cream if desired, and can be made well in advance because it freezes very well.

Serves 4–6

INGREDIENTS

3 pounds 5 ounces carrots
10 tbsp ghee
2¹/₂ cups milk
³/₄ cup evaporated milk or *khoya* (see
page 238)

10 whole cardamoms, peeled
and crushed
8–10 tbsp sugar

TO DECORATE:
¹/₄ cup pistachios, chopped
2 leaves *varq* (silver leaf) (optional)

1 Rinse, peel, and grate the carrots.

2 Heat the ghee in a large, heavy saucepan.

3 Add the grated carrots to the ghee and stir-fry for 15–20 minutes or until the moisture from the carrots has evaporated and the carrots have darkened in color.

4 Add the milk, evaporated milk or *khoya*, cardamoms, and sugar to the carrot mixture

and continue to stir-fry for a further 30–35 minutes, until it is a rich brownish red color.

5 Transfer the carrot mixture to a large shallow dish.

6 Decorate with the pistachios and *varq* (if using) and serve at once.

COOK'S TIP

A quicker way to grate the carrots is to use a food processor.

COOK'S TIP

Use pure ghee for this dessert, as it is rather special and tastes better made with pure ghee. However, if you are trying to limit your fat intake, use vegetable ghee instead.

Sweet Saffron Rice

This is a traditional dessert that is quick and easy to make and looks
very impressive, especially decorated with pistachios and varq *(silver leaf).*

Serves 4

INGREDIENTS

1 cup basmati rice
1 cup sugar
1 pinch saffron strands
1¹/₄ cups water

2 tbsp ghee
3 cloves
3 cardamoms
2 tbsp golden raisins

TO DECORATE:
a few pistachios (optional)
varq (silver leaf) (optional)

1 Rinse the rice twice and bring to a boil in a saucepan of water, stirring. Remove the pan from the heat when the rice is half-cooked, drain the rice thoroughly, and set aside.

2 In a separate saucepan, boil the sugar and saffron in the water, stirring, until the syrup thickens. Set the syrup aside until required.

3 In another saucepan, heat the ghee, cloves, and cardamoms, stirring occasionally. Remove the pan from the heat.

4 Return the rice to a low heat and add the golden raisins, stirring to combine.

5 Pour the syrup over the rice mixture and stir to mix.

6 Pour the ghee mixture over the rice and simmer over a low heat for 10–15 minutes. Check to see whether the rice is cooked; if not, add a little water, cover, and simmer.

7 Serve warm, decorated with pistachios and *varq* (silver leaf), and with cream if desired.

VARIATION

For a slightly stronger saffron flavor, place the saffron strands on a small piece of aluminum foil and toast them lightly under a hot broiler for a few moments (take care not to overcook them or the flavor will spoil) and crush finely between your fingers before adding to the sugar and water in step 2.

Ground Almonds Cooked in Ghee & Milk

Traditionally served at breakfast in India, this almond-based dish is said to sharpen the mind!
However, it can be served as a delicious dessert and is very quick to make.

Serves 2–4

INGREDIENTS

2 tbsp vegetable or pure ghee
1/4 cup all-purpose flour

1/2 cup ground almonds
1 1/4 cups milk

1/4 cup sugar
fresh mint leaves, to decorate

1 Place the ghee in a small, heavy-based saucepan. Melt the ghee over a gentle heat, stirring so that it doesn't burn.

2 Reduce the heat and add the flour, stirring vigorously to remove any lumps.

3 Add the almonds to the ghee and flour mixture, stirring continuously.

4 Gradually add the milk and sugar to the mixture in the pan and bring to a boil. Continue cooking for 3–5 minutes, or until the liquid is smooth and reaches the consistency of cream of chicken soup.

5 Transfer to a serving dish, decorate, and serve hot.

COOK'S TIP

Ghee comes in two forms and can be bought from Asian grocery stores. It is worth noting that pure ghee, made from melted butter, is not suitable for vegans, although there is a vegetable ghee available from Indian grocers and healthfood stores.

VARIATION

You could use coconut milk in this recipe, for a delicious alternative.

Indian Vermicelli Pudding

Indian vermicelli (seviyan), which is very fine, is delicious cooked in milk and ghee. Muslims make this for one of their religious festivals called Eid, which is celebrated at the end of Ramadan.

Serves 4–6

INGREDIENTS

¹/₄ cup pistachios (optional)
¹/₄ cup slivered almonds
3 tbsp ghee

1¹/₂ cups *seviyan* (Indian vermicelli)
3¹/₂ cups milk
³/₄ cup evaporated milk

8 tbsp sugar
6 dates, pitted and dried

1 Soak the pistachios (if using) in a bowl of water for at least 3 hours. Peel the pistachios and mix them with the slivered almonds. Chop the nuts finely and set aside.

2 Melt the ghee in a large saucepan and lightly fry the *seviyan* (Indian vermicelli). Reduce the heat immediately (the *seviyan* will turn golden brown very quickly so be careful not to burn it), and if necessary remove the pan from the heat (do not worry if some bits are a little darker than others).

3 Add the milk to the *seviyan* (Indian vermicelli) and bring to a boil slowly, taking care that it does not boil over.

4 Add the evaporated milk, sugar, and the pitted dates to the mixture in the pan. Simmer for about 10 minutes, uncovered, stirring occasionally. When the consistency starts to thicken, pour the pudding into a serving bowl.

5 Decorate the pudding with the chopped pistachios and flaked almonds. Serve the pudding immediately.

COOK'S TIP

You will find seviyan *in Indian grocery stores. This dessert can be served warm or cold.*

Almond & Pistachio Dessert

*Rich and mouth-watering, this dessert can be prepared
in advance of the meal. It is best served cold.*

Serves 4–6

INGREDIENTS

6 tbsp sweet butter
1 cup ground almonds
²/₃ cup light cream

1 cup sugar
8 almonds, chopped

10 pistachios, chopped

1 Place the butter in a medium-size saucepan, preferably nonstick. Melt the butter, stirring well.

2 Add the ground almonds, cream, and sugar to the melted butter in the pan, stirring to combine. Reduce the heat and stir constantly for 10–12 minutes, scraping the bottom of the pan.

3 Increase the heat until the mixture turns a little darker in color.

4 Transfer the almond mixture to a shallow serving dish and smooth the top with the back of a spoon.

5 Decorate the top of the dessert with the chopped almonds and pistachios.

6 Allow the dessert to set for about 1 hour, then cut into diamond shapes, and serve cold.

COOK'S TIP

This almond dessert can be made in advance and stored in an airtight container in the refrigerator for several days.

COOK'S TIP

You could use a variety of shaped cookie cutters to cut the dessert into different shapes, rather than diamonds, if desired.

Index

Index compiled by Hilary Bird.